estherpress

Books for Courageous Women

ESTHER PRESS VISION

Publishing diverse voices that encourage and equip women to walk courageously in the light of God's truth for such a time as this.

BIBLICAL STATEMENT OF PURPOSE

"For if you remain silent at this time, relief and deliverance for the Jews will arise from another place, but you and your father's family will perish. And who knows but that you have come to your royal position for such a time as this?"

– Esther 4:14

What people are saying about …

How'd I Miss That?

"Fun. Fresh. Faith-building. Cynthia Yanof reminds us that life with God isn't found in the big headlines but in the small, everyday choices. Forgive. Give generously. Love sacrificially. These are the choices that shape us into people who look like Jesus. *How'd I Miss That* will lift your eyes, fire up your faith, and leave you laughing along the way."

Louie Giglio, pastor of Passion City Church, founder of Passion Conferences, author of *Don't Give the Enemy a Seat at Your Table*

"Just like Cynthia Yanoff, this book is packed with personality, humor, heart, and wisdom. It made me laugh out loud and feel nostalgic for those days when life seemed simpler. Do yourself a favor and get this book. It will renew your outlook, elevate your hope, and fill your heart with joy!"

Kari Kampakis, bestselling author of *Love Her Well* and *Is Your Daughter Ready?*, host of the *Girl Mom* podcast

"Cynthia brings her all with this book—her charm, her wit, her wisdom. She will make you laugh, make you think, and help you navigate this wild and wonderful world in a Christlike manner. You will love her. You will love it."

Amy Weatherly, bestselling author, nationally
known speaker, co-founder of the Sister,
I Am With You online community

How'd I Miss That?

Gas Pump Confessions, Drive-Thru Obsessions, and Figuring Out What Really Matters

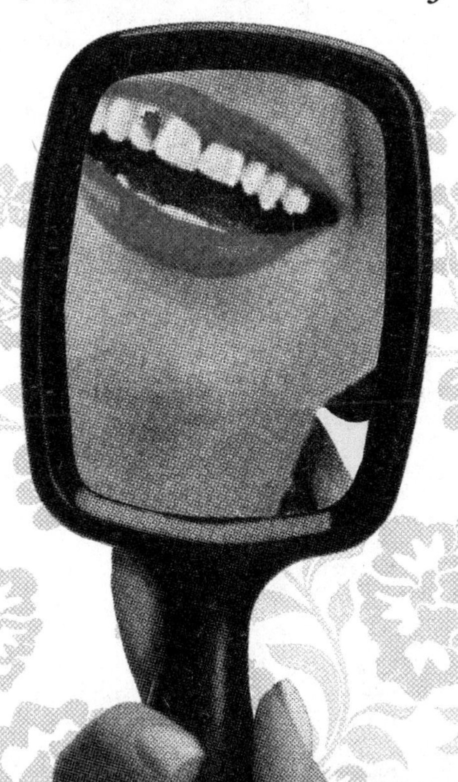

CYNTHIA YANOF

HOW'D I MISS THAT?
Published by Esther Press,
an imprint of David C Cook
4050 Lee Vance Drive
Colorado Springs, CO 80918 U.S.A.

A Ministry of Cook Media Global

Integrity Music Limited, a Division of David C Cook
Brighton, East Sussex BN1 2RE, England

Library of Congress Control Number 2025944065
ISBN 978-0-8307-8535-3
eISBN 978-0-8307-8536-0

The Team: Susan McPherson, Stephanie Bennett, Andrea Converse,
Judy Gillispie, Leigh Davidson, Susan Murdock
Cover Design: Leah Von Fange

Printed in the United States of America
First Edition 2026

1 2 3 4 5 6 7 8 9 10

110525

To Mike, Kate, Brett, and JB,

You're the best stories I'll ever tell. You live fully, faithfully, and hilariously. I may have missed a few things in my lifetime, but not once have I missed the gift of calling you mine.

Contents

Introduction

Why I Can't Be Left Unsupervised

I ran across this quote a few years ago that I haven't been able to get out of my head. It would be fantastic on a needlepoint canvas or maybe a crocheted item of some sort. But let's be real, I don't even know the difference between needlepoint and crochet, but my crocheting friends recently started referring to themselves as "hookers," so that's a whole situation. Nonetheless, here's the quote I love:

> There's very little difference between people—but that little difference makes a great deal of difference.
> *(unknown author)*

Isn't that the truth?

We've all encountered a person (or two or three) in our lifetime who is simply different from the rest. It's hard to pinpoint what makes them stand out because in so many ways they are just like us. There's no difference in what they wear, what they drive, or where they live. But the difference is much more than pedigree or geography; it's their life philosophy.

I'm reminded of a time when Jesus was talking about loving our neighbors and a lawyer asked Him to define exactly who constitutes our neighbor. (Bless it, lawyers—I get this, having once been a lawyer myself in the days of yesteryear.) Jesus responded by telling the story of a guy traveling from Jerusalem to Jericho who got beat up and left for dead on the road (Luke 10:25–37). (If hearing this story makes you think of *Monty Python and the Holy Grail* and you silently chant, "Bring out yer dead," please know you are my people.) A priest and a Levite saw him lying there but passed right on by without stopping to help. A Samaritan also came upon the injured man, but he actually stopped to care for this man's injuries and pay for a place for him to recover.

What was the difference in the people Jesus described in that story? It was some combination of outlook and availability. Each person had a unique outlook on the situation, and that outlook informed their actions. The robbers saw this Jewish man as a weakness to be exploited. The Levite and priest saw him as an obstacle to be avoided. And the Good Samaritan, despite Samaritans and Jews being bitter enemies, saw this broken and hurting man as a neighbor worth loving.

An outlook marked with compassion, mercy, interruptibility, risk-taking, availability, intentional living, and a willingness to serve others even when it's inconvenient can't help but inform our actions. That kind of mindset produces small pivots that significantly affect those around us. These things separate the men from the boys, or the crocheters from the needlepointers, so to speak. These are the *little differences* that make a *great deal of difference* in our faith walk, our parenting, our workplaces, and our friendships as we travel our own personal roads from Jerusalem to Jericho.

The roads we travel daily are where we encounter the broken, the hurting, and those desperately needing neighbors to act neighborly (hence Jesus' point), friends to act friendly, and Christians to act … well, Christian-ly. It could be the road between the partner's meeting and your desk, or between the gym and the carpool line, or the dorm and the intramural field. Or maybe it's the road from Dallas to Houston, which is a most unfortunate road because it holds my most recent embarrassing moment.

I was invited to speak at a women's event a few months back. It was a larger speaking event in Houston, so I was equally nervous and excited. Houston is only a few hours from where I live, so I decided to hit the open roads and drive rather than fly. An amazing group of friends often travels with me because they love to hear me speak. Except they recently told me they don't go because they love to hear me speak; they go because they think I'm marginally incompetent when it comes to travel logistics. So, there's that.

I let them know I was fine to drive myself to Houston, thank you, and off I went.

About halfway there, I stopped at Buc-ee's for gas and a Diet Dr. Pepper. Buc-ee's, you ask? Well, it's a Southern thing, and please let's not dare call it a gas station—that's heresy. Buc-ee's is a wonderland with treasures like brisket sandwiches, homemade fudge, and beaver-themed underwear. There are pickled quail eggs, sausages on a stick, and a 7.5 pound bucket of bacon grease with a sign above it that reads, "Great gift idea." Not even making this up.

An entire wall is devoted only to jerky, another display is filled with Buc-ee's onesies (one of which my husband weirdly owns and even more weirdly dons once a year on Christmas morning), and big ol' deer feeders are right around the corner from the fancy soaps and banana pudding. The bathrooms are pristine. Oh, and yes, Buc-ee's even sells gas.

Now I have no idea why the name Buc-ee's is hyphenated. Are they a product of divorced parents? Are they trying to keep name recognition for professional purposes? Some questions I cannot answer. But I do know that if loving Buc-ee's is wrong, I don't want to be right.

On this particular day, I was pumping gas when a lady and her young daughter approached me for help, saying they were hungry. I honestly had not one cent of cash with me to help them out, but they clarified that they needed food, not money. The usual questions ran through my head: *Is this a scam? Will this make me late for my important speaking engagement? Are they really hungry? Do they want my kidney?*

Skeptically and somewhat reluctantly, I grabbed a stash of snacks for the mother-daughter duo while I was inside the store. I handed them the bag upon returning to my car, and they thanked me profusely. Feeling like I was running behind at this point, I hurriedly jumped in my car to leave.

As I was driving off, I heard a loud *bang* behind me and slammed on the brakes. Only then did I realize that with all the chaos of buying snacks and safeguarding my kidneys, I forgot to remove the gas nozzle from my car. The hose was flapping in the wind with no pump in sight (and, no, it wasn't spewing gas because, apparently, we Buc-ee's folks do this with some regularity so it automatically shuts off).

Thankfully, I'm good under pressure, and I immediately knew what to do. Like when you fall down in junior high and in a split second have to decide if you're going to lay there and wail or jump up and act like nothing happened. I put the car in park and marched intentionally to the rear of my vehicle to remove the dismembered hose from my gas tank. Head held high, I walked the ten feet back to the pump, hose in hand, and returned the nozzle to its rightful place as if nothing even remotely strange just went down.

Now even for Buc-ee's standards, it got a little weird when I nervously stayed at the pump for a minute or two and randomly started punching buttons on the display screen. I mean what in the world? Was I trying to convince the twenty-plus eyes watching me that everything would be fine as soon as I finished handling some quick international business on that tiny little screen? Was typing away feverishly somehow supposed to explain away the idiocy of ripping that gas hose from the pump to kingdom come?

It's still a mystery why my friends don't trust me to travel alone. But here's the point—Jesus' point: Practically loving our neighbor means having eyes that are less fixed on the platform and more concerned with the needs at the pump. The ones who don't miss it know the moments that matter the most are often camouflaged in untimely delays, inconvenient asks, and even humbling course corrections.

Take a second to think about the people who have been most pivotal in your life. Those people who are ingrained in your story simply because of how they have lived. I think about my husband, Mike, my mom, my two dear friends Stephanie and Brandie, and several others whom you'll undoubtedly hear about in the pages of this book.

It's not their accomplishments that have marked me. It's not their leadership skills. It's not their political views, parenting successes, or social media posts. It's not really even their words. It's their availability, their steadfastness, their generosity, their grace, their loyalty, their kindness, their willingness to respect that I'm not a hugger, their quiet spirits, and especially their unwavering love for Jesus. It's the God-given few in our lives who will walk through the fire with us in our darkest hour—yet still interrupt our most profound thought with, "Girl, you've got the most heinous piece of spinach stuck in your teeth."

The Good Samaritan story ends with Jesus saying these four simple words: *Go and do likewise*. Both a challenge and a charge for reframing how we walk or, more realistically, how we travel in this life. A call to consider an outlook that worries less about how the world labels success and instead resolves to slow down, be kind, live less offendable, assume the best—making a difference by pointing others to Him rather than ourselves. It's doing the very things I had planned on doing before I got hooked on capsule wardrobe reels and then forgot why I went to the pantry.

And this is really what this book is about. Think of me as the friend who's willing to lean across the table and ~~discreetly~~ tell you there's food in your teeth. Not because I've figured it all out but because I've lived enough life with lettuce dangling from my smile (and gas hoses hanging from my car) to realize the things we so often miss—in our faith, parenting, friendships, marriages, and how we walk our daily lives—can carry eternal significance if we'll just let Jesus get ahold of them.

So my guess is that if we follow Jesus' instructions to *go and do likewise*, lives will be transformed—not the least of which is our own. And one day, when we're old and gray with bursitis and chin hair, we'll look back and realize that the moment-by-moment decisions of figuring out what really matters were the little difference that made a big difference.

Chapter 1

The Talk: A Cautionary Tale

The whole sex talk thing with our kids is dumb.

I hate to come out swinging on such a dicey topic, but it must be said.

There's virtually no conversation I shy away from—deep, shallow, marginally inappropriate, oversharing—except *the talk*. And honestly, the fact that we have to slap "the" in front of it like some ominous warning label should tell us everything we need to know. No other subject in life requires this level of verbal hazard lights.

Not once have I ever said, "Kids, we need to have *the talk* ... about new baseball cleats." Nor have I called my daughter over with, "Sweetie, come sit down. It's time for *the talk* ... about whether you want to live in the dorm or get an apartment next year." Nope. Only one talk in all of parenting carries such a weighty yet ambiguous title, and nobody I know thinks they've done it well. In a world where we outsource literally everything—from waxing our precarious parts to hiring someone to pick up our dog's poop—can we not just Venmo a professional for this one too?

One time, my young daughter was riding in the car with my very pregnant friend Stephanie, who noticed little Kate growing very quiet and concerned. Finally, Kate mustered up the courage to ask Stephanie, "Is there any way I'm pregnant too?" Stephanie immediately called me and demanded that I have *the talk* with my child. Naturally, I suggested Stephanie just go ahead and do it since, you know, the topic had already come up organically. She declined.

My two older kids are practically adults now, and they'll tell you, without hesitation, that no one is worse at *the talk* than me. So if you're one of those parents who actually gave your kids the talk and then proudly checked the opt-out box to prevent their lives from being ruined in a cafeteria full of peers learning the inner workings of reproduction—saying, "I want them to hear it from me"—listen, I love you as my Christian brethren, but you are not my people. (I was over here looking for the box that would let me opt my kids into the afternoon session too.)

Honestly, I don't help myself here. I've never been great with anatomically correct terms. I didn't realize how bad it was until I caught myself teaching my kids to refer to their bits and pieces as their "front bottom" and "back bottom." Somehow, that felt more respectable than *who-ha* and *tushie tush*, but only by the slimmest of margins. One night, I came home from a girls' night out and overheard my rule-following lawyer of a husband, Mike, course-correcting this disaster: "Okay, kids, Mommy was just kidding. Here are the real words ..."

Incorrect, good sir. I was not kidding. I was fully committed to using a more sanitized terminology.

I partially blame this on growing up in the purity culture of the '80s. Our parents were just as committed to avoiding *the talk* as we are, which meant youth pastors had to take one for the team. My pastor friend Steve still vividly remembers sitting in his youth group as their leader passed a white flower around the circle where fifty teenagers touched it, crumpled it, and generally destroyed it. At the end, the pastor held up the now-dirty, dismantled flower and dramatically announced, "This is what happens when you don't wait for your wedding night."

My three kids would have been sitting there stunned, asking, "Wait for what?" So now seems like as good a time as ever to apologize in advance to whomever marries my children. I did my best, and my best was clearly not good enough.

Neural Coupling: Where Brains Are the Only Thing Connecting

I bring all of this up because we should probably have *the talk*—you know, one of those conversations we all need to hear at some point in our Christian walk. Now, I'm also going to talk about seeds, and I'm a little worried you'll think somewhere between seeds and "the talk," I'm about to take a very awkward turn. So be assured, the version of "the talk" I'm giving is *not* the one you're thinking of, and hopefully, I'm better at this one than the one my kids are still waiting for.

My dad has always been a masterful storyteller. From my earliest days, I remember watching friends gather around whenever he would tell a story, captivated by the details and typically ending with peals of laughter. Yes, he's also funny, which is the perfect pairing for an already great storyteller. I learned at an early age the power of a story simply from watching my dad.

I inherited the storytelling gene, which is a matter of opinion I suppose, and whether that's a gift or just a polite way of saying I talk too much is up for debate. But one thing's for sure—I love hearing people's stories and I also love sharing my own. And it turns out, science is on my side. Research shows that storytelling isn't just entertaining; it actually fires up our brains.[1]

I recently read about neural coupling, a fancy term for what happens when the neurons in our brain sync up with someone else's while they're telling a story. It's also called mirroring, and here's why it matters: If I'm just rattling off facts or data, my brain and yours aren't really on the same page—literally. The part of my brain doing the talking isn't activating the same part of your brain that's listening, which is why you might start zoning out and thinking about writing a book someday titled *Broccoli's Never Made Anyone Fat*. Or maybe that's just me.

But the second I start telling a story? Boom!—our brains sync up, distractions fade, and suddenly, we're on the same wavelength. You've experienced it before without realizing it. Like when you're sitting in church, eyes glazed over, debating queso or guac at lunch—then the pastor starts a story, and suddenly, you're right back with him. That's neural coupling in action. It's not just storytelling—it's science (and probably a little Holy Spirit intervention).

Here's something else that's pretty fascinating: If you add visuals—pictures, demonstrations, or even vivid descriptions—while you're speaking, it significantly increases the listener's ability to remember what you said. Studies show that after three days, we typically retain only 10 to 20 percent of the information we hear or read. But throw in a visual? Retention jumps to 65 percent.[2] Which probably explains why my friend still remembers the white-flower wedding-night illustration from high school (or maybe we chalk that up to trauma).

Stories and visuals keep us engaged, which is more important than ever in today's world of smartphones and cat reels. They help us absorb and store information in a way that simple words alone just can't. And that's exactly why Jesus repeatedly used stories in His quest to provide the ultimate playbook on kingdom living. He was a master storyteller who didn't just list rules and say, "Hey, do this because it matters." Instead, He told stories with images that stuck and made sense to people in their own context.

On one occasion, Jesus had *the talk* with the disciples and others about the kingdom of heaven. He told story after story explaining the upside-down economy of following Him. One of my favorite stories He told was the parable of the mustard seed. Just two short verses, yet it's packed with meaning.

The parable goes like this:

> The kingdom of heaven is like a mustard seed, which a man took and planted in his field. Though it is the smallest of all seeds, yet when it grows, it is the largest of garden plants and becomes a tree, so that the birds come and perch in its branches. (Matt. 13:31–32)

Now picture this: A massive crowd had gathered—nothing unusual, since people would travel great distances just to hear Him speak. People crossed lakes, climbed trees, dropped down from roofs, and even skipped meals, all for a glimpse into who Jesus was. In this particular instance, the crowd had grown so large that Jesus got into a boat and preached from the water while a sea of people stood on the shore, eagerly listening.

He begins answering a question nobody is explicitly asking, but it's the elephant in the room for many in His Jewish audience in Galilee. They had always believed the kingdom of heaven would arrive with fanfare—trumpets blasting, a mighty Messiah commanding authority in packed synagogues, surrounded by the most powerful rulers of the day. They were not expecting a kingdom ushered in by a humble, common-looking man carting around a bunch of one-off disciples and giving sermons from the bow of a boat.

So Jesus tells a story that explains how big things of faith often come from small, humble beginnings. Yes, He's talking directly about His movement—but He's also talking about the small seeds of faith sown daily that are easy to miss and feel like nothing in the moment but have the capacity, through Jesus, to be profound. Tiny seeds with great potential.

Jesus wanted people to understand the *mustard seed mentality*: with Jesus, even the smallest acts of faithfulness have the potential for extraordinary growth.

Admittedly, the mustard seed imagery doesn't resonate as strongly with us as twenty-first-century Americans; today, maybe Jesus would reference the power in investing ten dollars in Apple stock back in the early '90s—a tiny seed of hope that would one day buy you a Bugatti. However, the crowd in Israel lived in a countryside dotted with mustard plants, and mustard seeds were scattered along the very paths they walked. To them, it symbolized something small, almost insignificant, yet capable of growing into something vast and transformative, and spreading far beyond where the original seeds were planted.

Jesus wanted people to understand the *mustard seed mentality*: with Jesus, even the smallest acts of faithfulness have the potential for extraordinary growth. In other words, the daily, seemingly insignificant steps of faith accumulate over time in ways we cannot begin to grasp—unseen, yet unimaginably powerful.

But there's also a trap in the mustard seed mentality, one that we fall into too easily. It's the mistake of assuming that if we don't see immediate results, then nothing is happening. It reminds me of bamboo. When you plant a bamboo seed, you often see nothing for nearly five years—just bare ground, no shoots, no progress. But beneath the surface, an intricate root system is silently forming, spreading deep and wide, laying the foundation for a skyrocketing forest. Then, almost overnight, bamboo shoots up at an astonishing rate, sometimes growing several feet in a single day.[3]

The *mustard seed mistake* is being bamboozled into thinking that if we can't see the growth—of our efforts, our prayers, our faith—then nothing is happening. But that couldn't be further from the truth. Jesus is actively working beneath the surface, cultivating deep, unshakable roots, all while preparing us for the moment when those hidden efforts burst into visible, undeniable growth.

All of that takes time. Sometimes lots and lots of time.

Mark Batterson says it this way: "We want things to happen at the speed of light. In the kingdom of God ... things generally happen at the speed of a seed."[4] So this is where I believe Jesus wants us all to have the talk with ourselves and with each other. Our job is to keep sowing the smallest seeds of grace, generosity, forgiveness, and love because a mustard seed mentality leaves the results to the only One who does immeasurably more than Apple stock or bamboo plants—even if it happens at the speed of a seed.

The *mustard seed mistake* is being bamboozled into thinking that if we can't see the growth–of our efforts, our prayers, our faith–then nothing is happening.

Throwing Shade

Many years ago, a dear friend became entangled in white-collar crime and was sentenced to ten years in prison. His wife and two children found themselves caught in the crossfire of his very public failure. In the midst of our heartbreak for our friend and his family, our pastor asked if he could share the situation with a few spiritual champions in our church.

One of those incredible people was Peggy Powell, an older woman in our congregation whom I had met a few times but didn't know well. She reached out to ask me for specific details about where our friend was incarcerated and how his family was doing, so she could pray with purpose and intention. What she did next was something nobody would have expected: every single day, without fail, she wrote him a letter.

For the eight and a half years our friend served in federal prison, Peggy wrote daily letters filled with casual conversation about her family, newspaper clippings she thought he'd find interesting, and questions about his family's well-being. There was no agenda, no expectation of a reply, and no overthinking about how he might receive the letters. She simply committed to write letters to a man she had never met, who lived in a different part of the country, and to pray for him and his family as if they were her own—because, as fellow believers in Christ, she knew they were.

It's nearly impossible to grasp the depth of selflessness in a woman who, day after day, sacrificially sat down, found the right words, bought a stamp, and mailed a letter. She even urged him to memorize Scripture, and together, letter by letter, they carefully wrote out passages of the Bible they were committing to memory.

Our friend told me that, during the darkest season of his life, Peggy made him feel seen and acknowledged. Though he had made a monumental mistake, she was his constant reminder that wholeness was still possible through Jesus.

For years Peggy prayed fervently over our friend's marriage and his children, asking God to protect them and heal their hearts from the deep pain and betrayal at the root of the situation. One day, several years into her letter-writing campaign, I had the chance to ask her what prompted such generosity and kindness. She gave me two reasons. Practically, she had heard that prisoners who received regular mail were treated better by the guards. Spiritually, she wanted him to know that he was far from forgotten but loved and forgiven in Christ. And this wasn't something she did just for my friend—but something she faithfully did for hundreds of prisoners over the years.

My friend finished serving his sentence and is back home with his wife and two children who are now young adults. He loves the Lord genuinely and remains incredibly sorry for what his crime did to his wife and children. However, at one point he told me that if incarceration was the cost of knowing Jesus the way he does now, then it was worth it.

Warren Buffett famously said, "Someone's sitting in the shade today because someone planted a tree a long time ago."[5] Generations of children and grandchildren will sit in the shade from seeds Peggy Powell planted for her brother in Christ letter by letter over eight long years, finally producing a visible bloom the day he returned home with his faith deeply anchored and his family intact.

Sweet Peggy Powell has gone home to be with Jesus, and I imagine that now, in the presence of her Savior, she sees it all clearly. She knows—without question—that the little things, like writing a simple letter day after day, far outlasted her time here on earth. You see, she embraced the *mustard seed mentality*. And now, on the other side of eternity, I believe she's witnessing the deep roots God has been quietly cultivating beneath the surface—roots that will one day bloom for all to see.

A Mustard Seed Mentality

Can we go back to neural coupling for just a second? I love that Jesus used stories to make a point because He wanted His audience to remember what matters. He could have just said, "In God's kingdom, small things eventually become big." But Jesus knew we probably wouldn't remember it. Putting a visual behind His words with a story meant that long after the crowd left the shoreline, His words would still be with them. Every time they walked by a field of mustard plants, or dusted a mustard seed off their sandals, or tasted mustard on their Ball Park hot dog (well, maybe not hot dogs for our Jewish friends), they would remember the truth Jesus shared that day from the boat.

I could easily just cut to the chase and say, "Love people well," "show grace," and "do hard things." Best-case scenario, you'll underline it with your trusty yellow highlighter and move on; worst case, you'll make a mental note that will be gone in a few days. But my hope is that every time you hear the name Peggy or buy a stamp or learn of someone incarcerated, you'll remember that small acts of daily obedience plant seeds that change lives and far outlive us.

So we've had *the talk* first thing out of the gate: small things make a big difference, and it takes a *mustard seed mentality* to keep going when the slightest bloom may be seven-and-a-half years in the making. But Jesus also said this kind of mustard seed faith moves mountains (Matt. 17:20). And I'm not sure about you, but some mountains need moving in my own life and the lives of my people.

So let's follow Peggy Powell's lead and commit today to remind those around us that they are anything but forgotten; they are loved and forgiven in Christ. And as you read the coming stories—both from my life and others'—remember that a picture is worth a thousand words (and neural coupling proves it). So don't miss it: let each story be a visual cue that the mustard seed mentality is the little difference that makes a big difference. Because you can bet your "back bottom" that one day, when you least expect it, those little seeds of faithfulness will bloom into something beautiful.

Go and do likewise.

Don't Miss It

- Planting mustard seeds is playing the long game. So is explaining human anatomy without using anatomically correct terms.
- Big kingdom impact rarely starts with a spotlight—it usually starts with a stamp.
- It's not the size of the seed that's the difference maker but the One who makes it grow.

Chapter 2

Beef Eaters and Brand Builders

I need to come clean with you on something.

The information I'm about to provide is not my effort at being sensationalistic. And I know some of you are going to be super disappointed knowing this about me, but it's my truth and it must be told.

I enjoy Arby's.

I find myself to be slightly apologetic about it until the moment I dip one of those seasoned curly fries into Arby's sauce and—insert chef's kiss—it's a little taste of heaven. Let's not forget the processed cheese product on top of the roast beef that has a shelf-life longer than my oldest child. Oh, and the onion roll brings tears to my eyes.

Now do I wish they would consider renaming their "Horsey Sauce" in light of the advertising campaign that revolves around the ambiguous statement of "we have the meats"?

Absolutely.

But it doesn't dissuade me from hitting the drive-thru a few times a year.

By myself.

In neighborhoods where I don't know anyone.

Thereafter disposing of my trash in back-alley dumpsters with the guilt of one disposing of a body after a heinous crime.

My kids think my Arby's affinity is uncharacteristically weird, saying it doesn't fit my brand. I can appreciate that; it's tough when you think you know someone—only to realize you really don't.

Brand Confusion

A few years ago, I had the chance to interview someone on my podcast, a person I'd admired for years for their incredible writing and speaking. They don't shy away from sharing their Christian faith and always challenge people to love others the way Jesus loves us. I was pinch-me levels of excited to have the chance to talk with them.

In the days leading up to the interview, my prep might have reached borderline obsessive. I studied less for the bar exam than I did for this twenty-five-minute conversation. Okay, not really. But I reread their books, stalked their social media, memorized their pets' names, and listened to their interviews on other outlets. I was ready.

The day of the interview finally came, and so did the nerves. I was equal parts giddy fan and nervous wreck. Since it was a virtual interview, I sat down at my computer a good hour early to triple-check everything from camera angle (no double chin, thank you) to flattering lighting.

When showtime hit and I logged into the Zoom link I'd set up, nobody was there. I waited. And waited. Then eventually I got a message from their agent: my guest was also on Zoom but somehow on a different link. I wish I had video footage of myself frantically scrambling to troubleshoot like my life depended on it. *How in the world was I on the wrong Zoom link when I created it for the interview?* Despite my most desperate efforts, nothing worked.

About fifteen excruciating minutes into this failed effort, I noticed a phone number I could use to call the guest directly. With my heart pounding, I dialed the number. As soon as they answered, I launched into a stream of apologies for this colossal disaster. The guest was understandably frustrated. They listened to what I had to say and then, very directly, let me know that they would not be rescheduling an interview with me now or in the foreseeable future.

I was devastated.

Yes, because I didn't get the interview.

Yes, because so much prep work went down the drain.

Yes, because I think my audience would have benefited greatly from this person's message.

But mostly because I thought I knew this person. I mean I didn't *know* them. But I knew their work. I knew their platform. I knew their faith. And I thought I knew what they were about. I was reminded of how confusing it can be when the way we act and the things we say don't align with the brand we claim.

As Christ-followers, our brand is love. Jesus spent His entire earthly ministry teaching His followers how to live with core values that pointed back to the bigger message of love. But Jesus did far more than just speak about love; He gave His life for it.

Gong Show Christianity

If you've been to many weddings, you probably think of 1 Corinthians 13 when love comes up in a biblical context. Also, if you were in a ridiculous number of weddings in the '90s like me, love also brings to mind unity candles, large bows on your back bottom, dyed shoes, and disposable cameras. Paul drops a hard truth in "the love chapter," noting that even if we do amazing things to help others but don't have love, it's nothing (loosely translated, obviously). He's defining the Jesus-brand of love: not flashy, not envious, not self-serving, but patient, kind, humble, trustworthy, and hopeful.

As if canceling out anything we do without love isn't a big enough kick in the pants—Paul tacks on the visual that actions without love amount to nothing more than the annoyance of a resounding gong or a loud cymbal. Now I'm no gong aficionado, but I do remember catching *The Gong Show* a few times as a kid at my grandparents' house. For the Gen Zers among us, *The Gong Show* was basically a low-budget kissing cousin to *America's Got Talent* and *The Voice*. Contestants would perform their various "talents" in front of a panel of celebrity judges who gave them scores ranging between zero and ten points based on their skill level (or lack thereof).

The best part was when the really bad acts not only received zero points, but they were also booed off the stage with the dramatic sound of a banging gong (picture a monkey playing a fiddle on the back of a clown being abruptly cut off by a huge brass gong). Now, if Paul were referencing *The Gong Show* in 1 Corinthians (which, of course, he wasn't, but you're welcome for the deep theology I'm bringing here), he'd say that even the best talent, sacrifices, and good intentions—without love—deserve zero points and a gong-filled ushering out the door.

Can we be honest here? As Christians, we have a long history of actions that are gong worthy. Let's look no further than the historic arguments over pipe organs, praise teams, politics, and the whole debate over the rightful place of women in ministry. Now, I'm not trying to stir up controversy (though I did just admit to liking Arby's, so what do I have to lose?), but here's the truth: we're sitting in churches filled with level-ten God-given giftings and blessings that risk netting out to zero points—because in all of our doing, building, and platforming, we forgot that love was the assignment.

Now, maybe I'm a glutton for punishment, but I can't help but wonder how our perspective might change if a gong crashed every time we convinced ourselves we were on brand doing the "right" or "Christian" things, but they weren't based in love.

It might go something like this:

- A "lifting her up in prayer" comment in a text thread where you're really just sharing gossip with a few friends. *Gong.*
- Correcting your spouse "in love," while listing his last ten mistakes. *Gong.*
- Posting a #blessed social media update to let *her* know your life is just fine without that friendship. *Gong.*
- Helping others once a month at a local ministry—but only to check the box for service hours. *Gong.*

- Giving 10 percent of your bonus with a forced smile because you really wanted a vacation. *Gong.*
- Holding babies in the nursery because the children's minister keeps cornering you. *Gong.*

Believe me, my toes are bruised and broken from this little litany too. But it's worth asking ourselves—if biblical love is wrapped in kindness, patience, humility, and sacrifice, would our daily lives be characterized as godly or would they be more "gong-ly"?

Fail Contracts, Pass Love

One of the first classes I took in law school was contracts. I was new to law school but historically a pretty good student, so I was ready to tackle this class. It was one of those classes where there were no grades other than the final exam. At the end of the semester, I studied like never before because I knew this grade was everything.

The day of the exam, I sat down at my desk, pen in hand (it was the old days, people), ready to dive into the first of two essay questions. As I skimmed through the questions, all the notes I'd studied and lectures I'd attended came rushing back, giving me more thoughts than I could possibly write in three hours. I knew my stuff.

When I finished, I felt good about it. With Christmas break ahead, I only had a few quick conversations with other law students about the exam before heading out. I vaguely noticed that the points I felt strongest about didn't quite match what others had focused on, but I just figured they didn't have the same contracts prowess as me, so that was unfortunate for them.

After Christmas break, the professor posted the test scores anonymously on the front doors of the law school. I anxiously searched for my student ID number. When I found my grade, the blood drained from my face. I had failed the entire class.

I couldn't meet with the teacher for a few days, so I subtly tried to gather insights from classmates about the test. Yes, those same classmates I had judged as not having my contract knowledge just weeks before. Devastatingly, I realized I had written my entire first essay on the *wrong plaintiff*. In other words, I answered a question that wasn't being asked and gave a completely wrong response.

When I met with my law school professor, he was genuinely shocked to learn that I was the student who had failed the test—since grading was anonymous. He noted how I always attended class. I had good input. Yet I was the *only one* who had failed. And honestly, I'm not sure if it made me feel any better when he told me that my essay would have been an A if the question I had answered was the one he was asking.

The entire class ultimately came down to one moment. It was one exam with one opportunity to show what I knew. I had read the books, attended the lectures, studied the outlines, and prepared for the very moment. But all the expertise in the world didn't matter, because it was misplaced. It all means nothing when you ultimately answer the question wrong.

There's a similar lesson in our faith. We can buy commentaries, attend Bible studies, join community groups, and even finish The Bible Recap in a year. But if our answer to our neighbor's questions about faith, Jesus, and eternity is based on anything other than love, we've failed.

Jesus made this same point when speaking to a lawyer in the Bible (who probably passed contracts on the first try—sigh). The lawyer asked Jesus to identify the greatest commandment, since there were 613 commandments total in the laws: 248 positive and 365 negative.[1] That was way too many for even a lawyer to keep up with, so he wanted Jesus to net out what really, really mattered. That very question had plagued the Pharisees for decades—what's the most important thing—and the lawyer wanted to get the answer right (while also probably trying to set Jesus up).

Jesus' response: "'Love the Lord your God with all your heart and with all your soul and with all your mind.' ... And ... 'Love your neighbor as yourself'" (Matt. 22:37–39).

Meaning, there's no use in ranking the importance of 613 commandments when, at the end of the day, only one matters most—love. It's not just the right answer; it's the whole answer. It's not just who we are; it's what we do. It's the standard by which we will be judged.

But it doesn't stop with just how we love God but also how we love others. The two go hand in hand. Similar to my contracts class, much of our Christian witness comes down to one-chance moments to have impact on those around us. Our tendency is to want to focus on the 613 theological points we take issue with in this culture, but Jesus cautions us to always answer in love.

Jesus understood that the world doesn't need more rules and rituals. It needs the kind of transformation that only real, genuine love can bring. He modeled it practically for us as He fed frustrated fishermen, touched hurting lepers, washed dirty feet, celebrated overlooked children, wept with grieving family members, extended mercy to the condemned, cared for the poor, and loved the orphans.

Love is woven into the small, daily acts of patience, grace, biting our tongues, and lending a hand.

His version of love is marked by less talking and more action.

Our youngest son, JB, loves to talk. I mean, he talks a lot. Sometimes when he's outtalked my patience, I'll get quiet in the car and stop responding. He will then say to me, "Too much talking?"

Our culture is asking questions about their worth, their identity, whether God sees them, and how to get through life when it's devastating. We have one-shot opportunities to answer these questions and point people to Jesus. If we're using lots of words with few actions, it might be an appropriate time to follow JB's lead and ask, "Too much talking?"

When the Light Goes Off

For years, I've been a huge fan of the *Today Show*. Not as much of a fan as I am of Arby's, yet still a fan. I vividly remember when Hoda Kotb decided to step away from her co-anchoring role with Savannah Guthrie to spend more time with her daughters. In the weeks leading up to her final day, the *Today Show* hosts paid heartfelt tributes to her with kind words and thoughtful gifts. But it was Craig Melvin (he replaced Hoda) who I believe shared the most insightful words about Hoda. He said:

"People in this business, when that little red light, it goes off, they're different people. We've worked with all these people before.

[Hoda,] you're the opposite. That little red light goes off, you are exactly like people see you in the morning."[2]

Who we are when the light goes off matters. The ones who don't miss it know that love is woven into the small, daily acts of patience, grace, biting our tongues, and lending a hand. They don't mistake applause for obedience and performance for love. It's a truth for whether we're helping our kiddos with math, volunteering at the church, or responding to a podcast delay that's completely off the rails.

If we claim to be about love yet act unloving, it will not go unnoticed.

And just as I can't promise that a life marked by love will get us recognized on the *Today Show* or celebrated by millions for our authenticity like Hoda, I do know this: if we claim to be about love yet act unloving, it will not go unnoticed. When our actions contradict our words, it's like preaching Whole30 to all your friends at the gym and then grabbing Arby's on the way home for dinner. (No judgment from me, BTW.)

Jesus said, "They will know us by our love" (see John 13:35). Love is our defining mark. Anything short of that then, much like my contracts exam, is answering the wrong question.

Don't Miss It

- Life is a series of one-shot moments to love people well—because they will know us by our love, or lack of it.
- Sometimes in the platform-building and reputation-protecting we forget the assignment is love.
- "Lots of knowledge. Zero execution. F." —My contracts professor on wrong answers, and Jesus on wrong loving.

Chapter 3

Sidelines and Scout Teams

My youngest kiddo is my favorite. I mean, not *really*, but as our two older biological kids often say, JB's the only one we chose. This little guy is hilarious, personable, and he's never met a stranger. He has the most incredible curly hair, which goes perfectly with his feisty personality. He's competitive, yet sensitive. He's fun-loving, yet inquisitive. He's adopted, yet a Yanof through and through.

He also struggles mightily in school.

Nothing comes easily for JB when it comes to academics. The journey has been, and will continue to be, difficult. And since I've been known to use my fingers when calculating a tip, he's definitely not walking this alone. School struggles are not a new road for our family because our older son, Brett, also struggled academically when he was in elementary school. I'll never forget the people who were difference makers for Brett along the way, like Jennifer Jobe. Calling her a tutor doesn't even begin to describe the way she championed him. She became a student of Brett, finding ways to love what he loved and learn how he learned. She reviewed his tests with his teachers, defended the reasoning behind his answers, and called me every time he had a learning breakthrough, with the most genuine excitement and delight. She truly "got" him.

Jennifer Jobe believed in Brett academically when it felt like nobody else did. She believed in who he was going to become one day, even when the rest of us weren't exactly sure how this would all play out.

We recently had a meeting at JB's public school to go over some extensive academic testing they had done. The results were, frankly, difficult to process. My husband, Mike, and I sat in that meeting, listening to the conference room full of educators talk about JB's struggles, while we all tried to remain positive and upbeat. At the end of this meeting, I decided it was a good time to say a few words to the team of people in the academic trenches with our precious son.

I told them about Jennifer Jobe and how she championed Brett all those years ago, acknowledging his struggles yet giving more weight to his strengths. I explained how she learned to think like he thought and taught him in ways that only made sense to him. I shared how her unwavering belief in Brett brought much needed hope and encouragement to me and Mike. Because everyone deserves at least one person who believes in them more than they believe in themselves. Someone who takes our setbacks and renames them as stepping stones on the path to success. And now, Brett is a senior in high school. He's been accepted to all four of the colleges he applied to and has even earned a congressional nomination to the US Naval Academy.

I can say with full confidence all these years later that Brett is where he is now, not in spite of the challenges he's faced but because of them. He just needed someone to believe forward, even when the times got tough, the path was untraditional, and the outcome felt unknown. He needed a namer.

As we ended that academic meeting for JB, I looked around the room and with tears in my eyes said these words: "I just need to know there are some Jennifer Jobes in this room."

Loudspeaker Lessons

Since we're being vulnerable about our struggles, it's a good time for me to share that there's a bit of a *situation* when it comes to me and sports. Picture the least athletic person you know. Seriously, take a moment and think about that person who would jump into the middle of a marathon conversation, only to assume it's a Netflix binge reference, not an actual footrace.

Got that person in mind? Great.

Now, I'm even less athletic than the person you're thinking of. Literally, not one Jennifer Jobe in the world could find a shred of hope in my athleticism (or lack thereof).

I share this because, in our household full of athletes, being the one unathletic person has been the thorn in my side. My husband played college baseball, and all three of our kids excel in multiple sports. My college daughter, Kate, even jokes that she's not dating to find her soulmate—but searching for someone with Division-1-athlete-baby-making potential. She's a real romantic, that one.

Not only are my people super sporty, but they are also real mean about it. Think back to being the last one picked for dodgeball in junior high (or maybe that was just me). Now imagine that happening at your kitchen table.

My son Brett has played football since his peewee days. If you've had a kid play football you can relate to where I'm headed with this; but only if you're a Texan can you truly appreciate the fanfare of Friday night lights. High school football in Texas is a religion of sorts. The TV series *Friday Night Lights* hit the nail on the head for Texas football (and I won't lie, Mike's been known to call me his Connie Britton, and in native Texas tongue that's akin to talking dirty to your wife).

Brett's sophomore year was supposed to be his football breakout year. He made the varsity team and was pumped. At the first game, Mike was giving high fives as the coin was tossed and the national anthem butchered. I was proudly wearing the mom jersey (which is everything I stand against) when I caught a glimpse of Brett on the sideline, stretching, with the unmistakable "Put me in, Coach!" look on his face. It felt like all his football dreams had come down to this very moment. And we were here for it.

How do I say this gently? We learned a lot about ending Friday nights with clean football uniforms and long, quiet car rides home after each game that season. Brett's sophomore year of *Friday Night Lights* came and went with him barely stepping onto the field, let alone making a tackle or recovering a fumble. (I take that back; he was a part of the drumline so he was on the field for the halftime performances. Bless it.)

After the season ended, we attended the football banquet. If you've never been to a football banquet, just know the highlight video is longer than the games themselves. District awards, team honors, and speeches, all of which go on ... and on ... and on. It's fine—unless you're sitting in the cafetorium, feeling horrible for your son who is disappointed and feels like a failure.

About nineteen hours into this banquet, the coach finally reached the last award. I was thanking Jesus for the light at the end of the inflatable football tunnel. Then, he called Brett's name and asked him to come to the front. *Umm, sir, you've surely got the wrong kid since this one scarcely touched the turf.*

The coach began to explain that Brett, along with a few others, was being awarded the Scout Team MVP. He went on to describe how the scout team players put in the same long hours, took the same hard hits, and endured the same blood, sweat, and tears as the starters. These boys had the same dedication and devotion as everyone else on the team, but when Friday night rolled around, they didn't actually play. In essence, their job was to get the *real* team ready for the game (my words, not his).

As he was handing out the Scout Team MVP awards, I realized this coach wasn't just handing out participation awards, instead he was handing out a valuable lesson I desperately needed to learn. The coach was taking my son's perceived football failure and naming it a success. He was redefining failure by teaching us that:

- Just because your name isn't called on the loudspeaker doesn't mean your contribution doesn't count.
- And just because you're not in the highlight reel doesn't mean your value is any less.

- And just because you play a supporting role doesn't mean your effort is a failure.

He reminded those boys—and, maybe even more importantly, their parents—that the road to success is often paved with *perceived* failures. That's why the struggle never gets the final word but perseverance, character, and grit do. Because the sidelines cultivate steadfastness and the bench breeds resilience. And I'll always be thankful for that Jennifer Jobe–style renaming moment (even if I developed a bedsore about five hours into that banquet).

The road to success is often paved with perceived failures. That's why the struggle never gets the final word but perseverance, character, and grit do.

Familiar Scout Team Members

God is the ultimate renamer.

He's constantly taking our perceived failures and naming them a success for kingdom purposes. He's calling us out of the crowd, out of our shame, out of our disappointments, and not just forgiving where we've fallen short—but celebrating the new road He has us on. He's applauding every ounce of our effort because He alone orchestrates our future, and He brings hope even when our dreams feel benched.

God gave David the ultimate Scout Team Award when He chose him—a young shepherd and the youngest of eight brothers—to be king. A reminder that while man looks at the outward appearance, God sees the heart (see 1 Sam. 16:7).

God gave Esther the Scout Team Award when He chose her, an orphaned Jewish girl with no royal lineage, to take on the title of queen. A reminder that His plans are bigger than our circumstances and He raises up the faithful, for a time such as this (see Est. 2:17; 4:14).

God gave Moses the Scout Team Award when He called this self-doubting, speech-impaired shepherd and fugitive to lead His people out of Egypt. A reminder that despite our doubts and limitations, God promises "I will be with you" (see Ex. 3:12).

God gave Rahab the Scout Team Award when He made her, a prostitute, a key player in His salvation story and secured a place for her in the lineage of Jesus. A reminder that no past is too broken for Jesus' redemption (see Josh. 2; Matt. 1:5).

I'm not sure what else to say if two murderers, an orphan, and a prostitute can't convince us that God's in the business of renaming our biggest setbacks.

When you dig a little deeper, you'll also see the unsung heroes in each of these stories, or, as I like to call them, the Jennifer Jobes. King David had Jonathan, Esther had Mordecai, and Moses had Aaron, proving that behind every success story—hidden humbly in the shadows of one's greatest moments—is a namer who has quietly advised, championed, believed in, and prepared the way for the "real team" to be game-ready.

I'm also guessing John the Baptist would have something to say about the humility and significance involved in preparing the way for the A-team.

Jesus applauds every ounce of our effort because He alone orchestrates our future, and He brings hope even when our dreams feel benched.

Starter or benched. Idolized or ostracized. Over and over God meets us right where we are, ready to pick us up, dust us off, and use us for His purposes. It happens most often in seasons where our kids have gone off course, our colleagues have passed us by, or especially when the metaphorical car rides have gotten very, very quiet. But right there is where God faithfully reminds us that no failure is final with Jesus.

Being a Namer

One of my mentors is Christian counselor Sissy Goff (although I'm positive she doesn't know it). In her office she has a sign with her favorite quote from Madeleine L'Engle's book *A Wind in the Door*:

> When I was memorizing the names of the stars, part of the purpose was to help them each to be more particularly the star each one was supposed to be. That's basically a Namer's job.[1]

Sissy told me she loves this quote because whether we're aunts, uncles, parents, grandparents, educators, friends, or neighbors, our holy calling is to help name those around us. To speak the truth of who they are until they start to believe it for themselves.

The namers in my children's lives will always hold the most sacred of places in our family. Being a namer impacts people that way. The reminder that God has renamed us allows us to do the same for others. We find ways to "pay it forward" by speaking truth into the perceived failures and struggles of others.

I'm guessing you can remember the namers in your life. Those who believed in you when you didn't believe in yourself. They encouraged you, defended you, and cheered for you against all odds. That's a namer's job.

By the way, I should tell you that Brett went on to be a standout football player the next season and played every down of every game until he graduated from high school. He has received multiple invitations to play college football and an NIL deal that has allowed me and Mike an early retirement.

JB has grown leaps and bounds academically. He's reading at a fifth-grade level (in second grade) while also participating in the gifted and talented program at his school. He even won the science fair!

Gosh, wouldn't that be amazing?

In reality, Brett quit football the next year after a frustrating series of injuries. It was a disappointing end to a sport that he poured his heart into for many years. But God made beauty out of his Friday-night-light ashes by teaching him the value of teamwork, sacrifice without expectation, and the importance of redefining success. And we're forever thankful for a godly football coach who didn't just value the superstars of the team but also renamed those who felt sidelined.

Precious JB is working harder than any kid we know. The gains are slow, hard-won, and often discouraging for him. Yet we're incredibly grateful for the team of teachers who are relentlessly championing JB.

The other night I was driving to one of Brett's last varsity baseball games when I received a call from Jennifer Jobe. Our sons play baseball together now and she wanted to let me know Brett wasn't feeling well—nothing urgent—but she'd already flagged the trainers and sent someone to the gas station to grab him some medicine. I thanked her and hung up and then just sat in my car, once again humbled. Because twelve years later—Jennifer Jobe is still standing in the gap for our son.

That's what namers do.

They don't just show up once. They don't check a box. They don't get too busy or lose interest or take the paycheck and move on. Instead, they quietly and intentionally lay foundations under our kids, friends, spouses, and colleagues who need help finding their footing. They text encouragement, drop off coffee, shed tears, spend the time, make the sacrifice, and over and over again pray deep and mighty prayers on our behalf to the Lord. They even cheer for others—the very ones they might be tempted to compete with.

You see, the ones who don't miss it understand that being a namer isn't just what you do—it's who you are.

And in a world that's loud with criticism and weary with comparison, we don't need more experts or influencers—we need more Jennifer Jobes. The ones who champion quietly and consistently, without needing the credit.

Don't Miss It

- The struggle never gets the final word—perseverance, character, and grit do.
- Behind every success story is a "namer" who has championed, advised, and cheered loudly from the sidelines.
- Some of God's best lessons come through banquet speeches and bedsores.

Chapter 4

The One Where I Admit I Don't Like "Friends"

I've decided my fifties are my favorite decade so far. My twenty-something-year-old self would probably hurl a fat-free SnackWell's cookie at me for saying that out loud—but it's true.

Admittedly, I'm not that far into my fifties, so let's leave a little room to amend this statement. Not to mention that my Amazon cart is telling a totally different story with the plantar fasciitis heel cups, the sleep gummies, the twelve-pack of readers, and the 10,000 BTU window unit I'm threatening to install solo if Mike doesn't crank up the dang AC.

Even so, I love my fifties. Maybe it's because I've finally stopped taking everything so seriously—except for the things that *actually* need to be taken seriously. Like colonoscopy prep, skin cancer checks (yeah, I'm looking at you '80s tanning with baby oil), and how much I dislike the show *Friends*. Wow, sorry to throw that out there so nonchalantly, but it feels inauthentic to keep that truth from you in a chapter on friendship. Not to mention I've got not even one more fake laugh in me for someone referencing "Smelly Cat" or asking, "How *you* doin'?"

The one thing, however, that worries me about the aging process is that I'll start to lose my inhibitions and say anything that comes to mind. I'm already a loose cannon, so the slow erosion of my internal filter? It's a major concern. It's probably time to lay hands on me or start a prayer chain or do something fairly significant because the older I get, the harder it is not to comment on the steady dose of irritants bombarding my days, like:

- People who say "any-who"
- Grown men who still fist-bump
- Teens who mock adults for calling it a "clicker" (you know who you are, Kate/Brett)
- Coffee invitations turned MLM "opportunities"
- People who say "literally" to figurative statements
- "Fur babies" in strollers
- Forwarded internet quizzes that identify your stripper name by combining the street where you grew up with your first pet's name (FYI: my stripper name is Esplanada Max, so it's *literally* a good thing I've got a day job.)

It's been my experience that in your fifties is also when you finally give yourself permission to not be everyone's cup of tea (wow, I just aged myself twenty years with that tea reference). And I've realized there's a world full of people who will love, strengthen, and sharpen us while pointing us back to Jesus. And a whole lot of people who will not. Friendships are among the greatest (and most fiercely fought-for) gifts this side of eternity. They've brought me more joy than anything in this world outside of my Savior and my family. Well, that's not completely true, there's also Diet Dr Pepper. And queso. And cooling mattress pads that keep you from sweating like a teenager about to post a new TikTok dance.

Competitive Swimming with a Free Side of Humility

Let me once again remind you that I'm the least athletic person you know. When I consider my unathleticism (surely that's not a word), one incident in particular comes to mind. A few neighborhood friends and I got a little ambitious a few years ago and decided to enter a mini-triathlon, because *obviously* if you have no athletic experience or talent, the next right step is a triathlon.

We picked a race for newcomers where the distances were shorter, thereby lowering cardiac arrest risks. If you're not a triathlete like myself (I *literally* laughed out loud writing that), here's a quick summary: swimming is first, biking is second, and you wrap it all up with a run. Oh, and they wear these horribly awful Dri-FIT onesies that leave nothing to the imagination. It's a real problem. Obviously, I opted out of the onesies; instead, I wore shorts and a T-shirt (think Champion brand, not even the sassy lululemon variety) thinking it didn't really matter—which, as it turns out, was the wrong move on every level.

The swim portion of this race was in a swimming pool, not open water lest we newbies drown. We had to give our estimated swim time when we registered so the race coordinators could group us with similarly skilled/unskilled athletes. Nobody needs a Michael Phelps wannabe blowing past sweet Susan and her kickboard (okay, those weren't allowed, but you know what I mean). Since my family has not been subtle in pointing out my lack of athleticism, I knew to slot myself in the *slowest* swim group with the lofty goal of not finishing dead last (or dead at all for that matter).

When I got in the pool that day, I noticed the girl directly behind me had only one leg. Now I realize this might be a bit insensitive to write about and 100 percent too honest—but we've come this far, so let's keep going (refer back to my internal filter issues). For better or worse, I felt a sense of relief seeing her behind me because I was pretty sure I could beat her on the swim portion of the race and, therefore, wouldn't be the very last one out of the pool.

It reminds me of when Mike and I took the bar exam after law school, and Mike said that in order to calm down before the test each day, he looked around the room and picked out four or five people he thought would fail (since every bar exam has several who don't pass). Picturing those four or five gave him confidence that he would pass because he would surely do better than those buffoons. For years, I've asked him to admit that I was one of the four or five he identified in that room to fail the bar—but he's a smart man and won't go there.

Swim cap on, I was ridiculously ready for my triathlon debut when the gun went off (okay, maybe it was just a whistle). My adrenaline was pumping, and I was swimming with the urgency of an Alcatraz escapee. With all the commotion and splashing, it was difficult to know where everyone else was, but I was pretty sure records were being set. I had even practiced the Olympic flip at the end of the pool in order to get maximum momentum but then thought better of it in the moment because sometimes I can't make the full rotation and end up like a dead cockroach stuck on my back.

I choose not to relive the exact details of what happened next, but somewhere around the time when I was swallowing copious amounts of water and perfecting my doggy paddle, karma paid me a visit—and I don't even believe in karma. Turns out the sweet girl slotted behind me had not only finished the swim but had also placed her prosthesis and taken off on her bike before I even had the chance to burp up some pool water and take off my goggles.

That should have been the beginning and end of my triathlon career, folks. Grab the T-shirt. Post picture of me biting the medal. Walk to the car with my tail between my legs and pray my friends never realize exactly how it all played out.

The end.

Signing Up for a Triathlon Doesn't Make You a Triathlete

I've met exactly zero women who wish they had *fewer* friends. Not once have I sat down for coffee with someone who says, "You wanna know my life's struggle? Too much support and connection." We all crave deep, meaningful friendships—loyal, steady people who stick around when the road gets rocky. And sure, we wouldn't mind if they were also witty, stylish, lived across the hall, and met us daily at Central Perk after splashing around in a fountain with umbrellas and a rogue living room lamp. (For the record, I never said I haven't watched the show.)

We rarely pause to think about friendship—until we really need it. Like when we're dying to share a hilarious story but not sure who to call. Or when life blindsides us with hard news and we're wondering who will help carry the weight. Maybe our marriage hits a rough patch and we find ourselves questioning who's safe enough to trust. Or perhaps the kids are grown, the house is quiet, and we suddenly realize that somewhere in the chaos of carpools and calendars, our closest friendships slowly drifted away.

You've probably felt it at some point: that gnawing ache of disconnection. I resonated deeply with Jennie Allen in her book *Find Your People* when she confessed that after spending so much time writing a book about friendship, she suddenly realized she felt isolated and unsure if she had any real friends left. She felt like a fraud. I get it. Maybe you've been there too—caught up in the busyness of life, distracted by all the demands, and then one day it hits you: I think I've lost my people.

The good news is we've all been there. We were created for connection. Yet so often we have an idyllic and/or naive notion of what it takes to fulfill the very thing we were created for. We want next-level community like *Friends*, but convince ourselves that it must just come naturally for everyone else. We start to believe narratives that we're not extroverted enough, or funny enough, or interesting enough, or not [fill in the blank] enough.

Just as registering for a triathlon didn't make me a triathlete (understatement), forming deep, quality friendships doesn't come with superficial, convenient, barely-showing-up efforts. I'll be honest—I wanted the triathlete title without the training, discipline, clean eating, or gear that would've made the experience even remotely bearable. And I've done the same thing with friendship. I've craved real connection without committing to the intentionality, the showing up, the vulnerability, the forgiveness, the persistence when it gets messy. I wanted the reward without the work and learned the hard way that friendships—like triathlons—don't just happen.

Just as registering for a triathlon didn't make me a triathlete, forming deep, quality friendships doesn't come with superficial, convenient, barely-showing-up efforts.

Incidentally, if you went to Vacation Bible School at any point in your childhood, you inevitably heard a lesson on friendship. You also ate Goldfish with Hawaiian Punch, sang "Father Abraham," and competed in one-legged races in the scorching sun (which seems insensitive now that I think about it). One of the standard VBS lessons on friendship comes from Jonathan and David. Jonathan protected David from his own dad, Saul; gave David his robe and armor; and humbled himself to honor David as the future king—even though Jonathan was supposed to be the king.

What seemed like great friendship lessons for kids all those years ago also turns out to be great friendship lessons for adults. And just in case you didn't attend VBS ... every ... single ... summer for ten years (which sometimes felt like twenty years crammed into five days)—here are a few solid takeaways. Real, authentic friendship looks like:

- Celebrating someone's success, even when they get what you wanted
- Keeping their name safe in rooms they're not in
- Being generous enough to give your best—your time, your energy, your "armor"—when it seems there's barely enough to go around
- Championing them when others are not
- Supporting their calling even at the cost of your comfort
- Knowing when an opinion is helpful/necessary and also when it's not
- Having the wisdom to realize that not every friendship is healthy in every season (okay, this is more of a Cynthia truth than Jonathan and David's)

Second-grade Cynthia naively thought most of those VBS friendship lessons would come naturally and went without saying (i.e., so let's move on over to the snow cone portion of the day). But fifty-year-old Cynthia has watched friendships end over youth sports and playing time, snarky group texts, room-mom drama, girls' trip invites (or lack thereof), parenting disagreements, mismatched vacation budgets, passive-aggressive Instagram posts, political opinions, side texts, fighting for control, assuming the worst, forcing yourself into a room you weren't invited into, and yes—not liking the show *Friends* (kidding ... mostly). I'd say a good two-thirds of those friendship enders could have been eliminated if we'd only been listening in VBS instead of worrying about potentially taking a ball to the face during rec time.

On a sidenote, it wasn't just Jonathan who taught us something about friendship. David did too. After Jonathan died, David sought out Jonathan's disabled son, Mephibosheth, and brought him to live with David. He didn't just give him basic care, he gave him a seat at his royal table (2 Sam. 9). That's the appropriate response to real friendship—it's making a seat at the table for your friends, their kids, their baggage, their shortcomings, and even their deficits.

At the end of the day, we're all racing with some kind of limp. Sometimes it's visible like the girl swimming ~~behind~~ in front of me. But more often, it's the invisible kind—self-doubt, fear, jealousy, bitterness, a loop of comparison or criticism that plays on repeat. It takes real courage to decide you're not going to bag it in and settle for a participation medal. It's the daily choice to make the call, plan the lunch, get uncomfortable, cheer them on, listen without judgment, and show up even when it feels hugely inconvenient and impossibly vulnerable.

That's the appropriate response to real friendship—it's making a seat at the table for your friends, their kids, their baggage, their shortcomings, and even their deficits.

Who You Run the Race with Matters

Hands down, the best part of doing my one and only triathlon was having my friends alongside me. The worst part? Riding a bike with wet unmentionables (the awful Dri-FIT onesies suddenly make more sense), followed by running a few miles with legs that felt like hundred-pound bags of cement. Also, am I the only one wondering why they don't hand out chafing gel with those tiny water cups at the race stations? But I digress.

My friends and I made memories that will live in infamy. Like when Tracy's bike chain fell off mid-race and I *blew past her* because I was too busy chasing my swimming nemesis. Or when Jenni came in dead last because it started raining and she was deathly afraid of falling off her bike. Or when one friend (who will remain nameless) just straight-up bailed on the race because she overindulged at the local Mexican restaurant the night before (a story for a different book).

When the rain comes, the chains fall off, or your judgment is clouded—you're gonna want the right people beside you. That's why it's critical we choose wisely.

When my kids were in elementary school, one of their big projects was called the Wax Museum. Each student dressed up as a person who changed the world in some way. It didn't have to be someone as serious as Gandhi or Bonhoeffer or Florence Nightingale—but it was also frowned upon to dress up like Will Ferrell holding a cowbell. (Which, for the record, I believe would've been iconic.)

My son Brett chose Bono, the lead singer of U2 and a global humanitarian. Let's call this exhibit A of the amazing parenting happening over here. (Oh, and exhibit B is that my kids can quote a *Seinfeld* line for virtually any life event. My podcast guest is boring? They snarkily tell me it's "a show about nothing." A grandparent says something politically incorrect at Thanksgiving lunch? Simultaneously, they chime in with "not that there's anything wrong with that.")

When I walked into the school and looked around the room, there he was—Bono in full glory. Leather jacket, sunglasses, chunky boots, guitar slung over his shoulder. Like the real wax museums, he sat frozen until you pressed the pretend little red button in front of him. Then, with great seriousness, he launched into his speech about forming a band with his high school friends, getting inducted into the Rock and Roll Hall of Fame, and being nominated for multiple Nobel Peace Prizes. And then Brett went back into his frozen mode until the next person pushed the button.

Standing there, surrounded by a room full of tiny world changers—some groundbreaking, some pop culture, and some unrecognizable because I'm really bad at history—I realized something: Yes, Bono and Bonhoeffer and Florence Nightingale changed the world. But when I think about who has changed *my* world, it's not Nobel laureates, rock stars, or humanitarians. My wax museum is filled with dear friends like Brandie, Marianne, Stephanie, Noel, Danylle, Kristy, Sherry (even with her new cat fetish), the Wednesday Lunch Crew, my parents, my husband, and a lot of others who rarely make headlines—but always show up.

In my wax museum, you'd walk through and push their little red buttons and hear incredible stories of faithfulness, friendship, sacrifice, big wins, great kids, hilariously embarrassing moments, weekly lunches, and an epic couples' trip to Santa Fe to look at an overrated staircase. But you'd also hear about the hardships like grown kids with big struggles, years spent wrestling through childhood trauma, learning differences, career dreams that didn't pan out, marriages that almost didn't make it, prodigal children they're still praying home, body image hang-ups, and seasons where the only thing holding it all together was a thread ... and Jesus.

It's not just my story; it's all of ours. A room full of the faithful, the broken, the forgiven, the ones who just kept showing up. That's the complicated and beautiful picture of true friendship.

We all want connection.

We all want to find our people.

But make no mistake, you and I look like the people who are shaping us. That's why it matters who we run our race with.

On my good days, I look a lot like my friend Brandie—kind, patient, and someone who shows glimpses of Jesus to every child she teaches. Other days, I look like Marianne, who's fashionable, fun, and lives with the kind of joy every Christian should carry. Some days, I channel Stephanie, with her deep wisdom and insatiable hunger for time with the Lord. Then at times I resemble Noel—a wise mother whose godly confidence encourages me to keep fighting for the things that really matter in our family.

Yet I can also remember days when I didn't look like those friends. The roomful of people influencing me were critical, impatient, reactive, insecure, exclusive, and gossipy. To be clear, it's not that those people aren't worthy of my love. Fearfully and wonderfully made? Absolutely. But if I'm going to be clothed in compassion, kindness, humility, gentleness, and patience (Col. 3:12), then my wax museum needs to be full of people who show me how to live that way.

Eat. Love. Pray.

Here's an epiphany I've had in my fifties: Most of my friendships revolve around food. (Oh, and the realization that I'm gonna need people to stop telling me what they dreamt last night because, respectfully, nobody cares that you decorated a Whataburger with Laura Ashley curtains while singing "Tiny Dancer." #NoFilter) But back to friendship and food. Honestly, if you throw a taco in front of me, I could probably bond with a ventriloquist's puppet. Refer back to my Wednesday lunch girls, my "besties" birthday dinner crew, and several Mahjong groups who refuse to start a game without a tray full of snacks—basically, if it's edible, it's eligible for my calendar.

But I meet with two particular friends every so often for one sacred ritual: biscuits and gravy. We go to a little dive in my neighborhood called Norma's. It's home cooking at its finest—greasy, buttery, and our favorite version of farm-to-table (mainly because it completely ignores the entire concept of farm-to-table). We drink an ungodly amount of Diet Dr Pepper and not a one of us dares to suggest it might be time to switch over to water.

The agenda for each get-together is to discuss one thing: why we can't lose weight. We blame genetics. We blame hormones. We blame our thyroids. We even blame stress, kids, work, and the rebellion our bodies have staged after years of SlimFast shakes and Weight Watchers weigh-ins.

But you know what we *never* blame?

The biscuits and gravy.

Because here's the truth: It's never really been about losing weight (which is probably self-evident). It's more about reminders that we have people in our corner, willing to sit and listen rather than judge and advise. It's about having friends who understand that we'd rather talk about biscuits than bills and aging parents and finances and the impossibly hard parenting battles we're facing.

Yes, we pray for each other often and fervently.

Yes, we speak hard truths that we'd rather not address.

But never at Norma's.

Because some days, you don't need a sermon; you just need someone across the table, nodding knowingly and saying, "Hormones, girl. It's definitely the hormones," as they quietly slide the gravy bowl back your way.

These are the people I want in my life and yours. That's why it matters who we run the race with and how we approach our friendships. Because the ones who don't miss it understand there's nothing better than having friends who know when to talk, when to listen, when to laugh, when to pray, when to cry, and when to head to Norma's.

Don't Miss It

- You don't stumble into real, deep friendship; you build it intentionally and vulnerably.
- Most times the best friendships are built over biscuits and gravy, not sermons and advice.
- You become like the people you walk with. Choose wisely.

Chapter 5

Adopted, Accepted, Occasionally Flatulent

Our youngest son loves books filled with bizarre facts. You know, the kind of books littered with random stuff about the human body, animals, the universe, and anything and everything that nobody really knows about (and truly I'm not sure anyone over eight years old really cares about either). And yet, there's something mysterious about these random facts that seem to capture kids' attention.

And you know what else is mysterious? Why I'm about to share a few of these fun facts with you. So perk up and grab your trusty highlighter because I've got some critical information coming your way.

1. Scientists have found that rats giggle when they are tickled.[1] I'm less stunned by the fact that they giggle and more concerned for the scientist who one day decided, "Hey, let's give it a try and tickle a rat."

Like was this an agenda item at a scientists' daily meeting by which the newbie in the lab drew the short end of the stick and had to start tickling the lab rats? Or was it more of a cloak-and-dagger situation on a Friday afternoon when a lonely scientist with no weekend plans thought, *Why not? These rats have become as close as friends; let's play a little tickle game.* Either way, it's weird and wrong and maybe criminal.

2. You flatulate during colonoscopy procedures.[2] Excuse me?! As if hitting the age where *shopping at Chico's* and *crossing my legs when I sneeze* wasn't humbling enough, now I must come to terms with *this* news? It took me a decade of counseling to recover from learning you might poop while giving birth. (Thank You, Jesus, for two C-sections; but I stand in solidarity with those of you who did in fact poop.) But here they spring it on me that while I was peacefully sleeping with a long tube up the buttocks, air was sent through my bowels thereby resulting in me potentially blowing one doctor and three nurses right out of the room? Back to counseling.

Before I go any further, I need you to know that I'm limiting myself to only one more weird fact—and it's not because I ran out of material—but because I'm showing restraint. (Or my editor shut me down. Either way.) But just know that I could have gone on for days about the chicken that lived eighteen months without a head, the fact that chainsaws were originally invented for childbirth (yes, you read that right), or that 1 in 18 people is born with a third nipple.

Oh, and I learned that the proper name for the fear of long words is *hippopotomonstrosesquipedaliophobia*. Which is a cruel joke, but also—objectively—hilarious.

Okay, this *really* is my last strange but true fact:

> **3. Humans can't walk in a straight line without a reference point.**[3] I experienced this firsthand at a Christmas party game night when each of us was blindfolded and told to march in place for precisely sixty seconds inside a circle taped on the floor. I was completely convinced I hadn't moved an inch. I was steady as I stood there marching with absolute precision, reminiscent of my high school marching band days (which are for me to know and for you to not make fun of). I owned that taped circle. But then they took off my blindfold, and I was nowhere near the circle. I had wandered over to the Christmas tree and was marching in tiny, delusional circles like a lost Roomba.

The Story of Us

I have a dear friend, Dee Dee, who, like me, had much older children before answering the call to adopt from the foster care system. Her two youngest children came from a difficult past, moving between their biological home and their now adoptive family, with CPS involvement woven into their earliest years.

Still being very young, her children had some idea of their background but not the full story. Dee Dee sensed the Holy Spirit telling her to share their entire story, which included revealing that her children have a half-brother. She sought to relay this information age-appropriately and came up with an idea.

One of her grown daughters is an artist, so she asked her to make paper-doll inspired drawings of each of the family members, including the biological mom, biological grandmother, adoptive mom and dad, adoptive siblings, and adoptive grandparents. She also made drawings representing each of their houses and color-coded them with the individual(s) who lived there. She made drawings representing the towns where the adult siblings lived now, and even a drawing pinpointing where Dee Dee and the kiddos live in the state of Texas.

One evening, just before bath time, Dee Dee and her husband, Brian, gathered their two adopted children and spread out the laminated drawings on the floor—each one a symbol of their children's past. The kids sat, eyes wide, absorbing the images as their parents began to tell a story that would be both painful and redemptive. Knowing that to move forward confidently their children had to understand their full identity, they began the conversation with these words: "This is the story of us."

As she shared this with me, it hit me that Dee Dee's precious children aren't the only ones who need to know their backstory. You and I also have a story—one that is challenging and profoundly redemptive. It's a story that reveals the true depth of our identity and serves as our reference point—keeping us from walking around in proverbial circles like I did on game night last Christmas. Now if you think I'm about to give you the same tired identity talk covered in countless books every year, please know—I am.

But writing a book about what *really* matters without considering "the story of us" is an invitation to spend your life walking around in circles like a chicken with your head cut off (which you now know can actually happen). I'm passionate about knowing our identity because I've seen firsthand how clearly it shapes the way we live each day. When we know who we are in Christ, we're able to step into what He's called us to do—with confidence and purpose. Read that again: When we know who we are in Christ, we're able to step into what He's called us to do—with confidence and purpose.

And, conversely, not living in the complete freedom of knowing who we are in Christ comes at a huge cost—a cost that impacts not just our own lives but also the lives of our family, friends, neighbors, and countless others in our culture who desperately need to know Jesus' grace and salvation. Don't miss this: If we don't know who *we are*, it's really hard to show the world who *Jesus is*.

So just like my friend did with her precious adopted children, I invite you to sit with me, metaphorically, on the rug. Let's look at the images of our past, vividly drawn through every page of Scripture, from Genesis to Revelation—and see how this is the story of us. And I understand it will take a little gumption to stay with me on this identity journey through the Bible—but let's take it slow and I promise not to use big words for those of you struggling with *hippopotomonstrosesquipedaliophobia*.

Not living in the complete freedom of knowing who we are in Christ impacts not just our own lives but also the lives of our family, friends, neighbors, and countless others in our culture.

Genesis, Exodus, Leviticus

From the very beginning God shows His love for us by creating us in His image. He draws up a covenant with Israel (that was really a covenant with Himself because He knew He was the only reliable party), and despite their shortcomings, gives them the Law—showing that holiness leads to a deep, abiding relationship with Him.

Numbers, Deuteronomy, Joshua

God's love for His people is shown through His faithfulness, grace, and deliverance, even as His people continue to run kicking and screaming from His commandments. He demonstrates His heart for i-m-p-e-r-f-e-c-t leaders, using them for great purposes while offering grace on the way to the Promised Land.

Judges, Ruth, 1 & 2 Samuel

From the chaos of everyone doing "what was right in their own eyes" (spoiler: it wasn't right) to the quiet faithfulness of Ruth and the rise of kings, these books show God working through unlikely people and less than optimal situations. Even when His people forgot Him, He never forgot them. God loves us enough to use broken systems and broken people to carry out extraordinary plans.

Kings and Chronicles

We see God's love revealed in His covenant faithfulness, even as Israel suffers the consequences of sin. Old kings, new kings, child kings, and worse-than-Jezebel kings rise and fall, but God lovingly calls His people to repentance and restoration, showing mercy in the midst of judgment.

Ezra, Nehemiah, Esther, Job

Despite exile, opposition, and personal tragedies, God's love remains the constant thread through it all. Whether He's rebuilding walls, saving queens, or even allowing His people to go through tough times to teach them important lessons—it's a narrative that even when "life is messy, God is good." (Someone should write that book too.)

Psalms, Proverbs, Ecclesiastes

God's love is revealed through His presence in both joy and sorrow, His wisdom, and even in our questions about life's meaning. He offers the only lasting and faithful love—steady in a world that feels wobbly. Everything else is just *hevel* ... it's meaningless.

Major and Minor Prophets

Through warnings, visions, and more than a few dramatic object lessons (we're looking at you, Ezekiel), God continued to show that He never gives up on His people. The prophets called out sin, begged for repentance, and pointed to hope in the midst of hopelessness. God's love is relentless, His justice is real, and He is always making a way back to Himself—even when His people are ridiculously stubborn.

The Gospels

God's love is unmistakable through the life, teachings, death, and resurrection of Jesus. In each of the four Gospels, we see a love that heals, teaches, and forgives—and sometimes even comes with a little bit of table-turning theology.

Paul's Letters

Paul makes it clear that God's love is the ultimate gift—salvation that we don't deserve and can't earn. He reminds us that our faith is all about unity, humility, and loving others (even the difficult ones, ahem, Corinthians). Over and over we see that nothing can separate us from God's love. Nothing.

Hebrews, James, 1 & 2 Peter

We're reminded that living in the fullness of God's grace isn't just a suggestion but an open invitation based in Jesus' deep love for us. His sacrifice is our all-access pass to God, and we're called to show our love for Him by loving others. We can make it through the bumps in the road because God's love is the foundation for steadfast living.

1, 2, & 3 John, Jude

God's love is the ultimate guide to living well and loving others. Since God is love, if we want to follow Him, we need to love like He does (sorry, no loopholes). There will be false teachers and people who make things harder than they should be, but Jesus provides protection and perseverance. That's what love does.

Revelation

The final victory over evil is God's ultimate declaration of love. Amid the trials, tribulations, and wild imagery, the core message is clear—God wins. Evil is defeated, and a new heaven and earth await. Jesus has already secured the victory, and one day, there will be no more pain, no more tears, no more death, and no more giggling rats. Now that's what I call the ultimate love story.

I know that was a lot, but did you catch it?

Don't miss how the entire Bible, from Genesis to Revelation, tells a profound story of God's love for us. It's the very essence of who we are. If it's true that humans can't walk in a straight line without a reference point, then knowing our identity in Christ is our spiritual reference point—keeping us from walking around in circles trying to figure out who we are and our purpose. Although our earthly days are both redemptive yet hard, we are covered in the unblemished love of Jesus, who has already determined our worth. He chose you as an adopted child into His family and, before you took even one single breath, had specific kingdom plans designed for you. He has not only declared that you are enough but that you are a key player in His plan to save the world.

The concept of adoption is critical to understanding our identity, and one our family had a front-row seat in experiencing.

JB's Gotcha Day was November 21, 2017. That's the day we stood before a judge, we signed papers, and in a matter of moments, he became legally and forever ours. The courtroom was packed with friends and family who came to celebrate what God was doing in JB's life—and in ours. It was joyful, emotional, and honestly, a little chaotic (because managing a toddler in a court of law isn't ideal for anyone). But it was unforgettable when the judge issued a brand-new birth certificate to our son. A new name. A new legal identity. A new family. The old document? Invalid. Erased. No longer the sum of his story.

That's exactly what happens when we give our lives to Jesus.

We are made new in Christ (2 Cor. 5:17). Our old identity—marked by sin, shame, and striving—is no longer who we are. We get a new name (Rev. 2:17), a new inheritance, and a new Father. We don't earn our place in the family, we simply receive it through God's grace—just like JB didn't earn his adoption by being good enough or making promises to always make his bed and one day become a D1 pitcher (although you and I both know Mike's working on that).

If it's true that humans can't walk in a straight line without a reference point, then knowing our identity in Christ is our spiritual reference point–keeping us from walking around in circles trying to figure out who we are and our purpose.

But here's what I've learned from parenting an adopted child: identity isn't dictated by behavior. There are days when JB talks back, disobeys, and/or storms off in frustration. But we don't go digging through the safe to find the old birth certificate because his adoption has been undone by his behavior. Why? Because the old one is not valid. His identity is sealed—no matter how he acts, how he feels, or how long he needs to come back around. He is ours. We would have it no other way.

And so we are, in Christ. Long after the emotional high of salvation fades, and the crowd is no longer gathered, we are still His. Adoption into God's family isn't a temporary emotion; it's an eternal position. It's not based on performance or appearance. It's based on a blood-bought sacrifice, signed and sealed by the Spirit (Eph. 1:13–14).

Just as Gotcha Day was only the beginning of JB's story with us, salvation is just the beginning of our story with Jesus.

The Question Is Already Answered

The following night, just before bedtime, Dee Dee's children asked once more if they could go through the drawings and hear "the story of us." Dee Dee, thrilled that they asked, settled in to retell it. But to her surprise, her son looked up at her and asked, "Would it be okay if I told the story this time?"

Without a moment's hesitation, he began recounting the story, just as he had heard it the night before. He didn't flinch at the painful parts—the parts of the story no child should ever carry. But when he reached the moment when CPS called Dee Dee and Brian, asking if they would take the children back into their home and adopt them, this sweet little boy's words were simple, yet profound: "When CPS called, they didn't even finish the question—your answer was already yes."

No matter the doubts you carry about your past mistakes, your worth, or your qualifications to belong to God's family, don't miss this:

before you even ask the question, Jesus has already answered with an unshakable, unqualified "yes."

You are His.

You are loved.

You are redeemed.

You are worthy.

You are a critical part of His eternal plan of salvation for all people.

This, my friends, is the story of us. And now, with a broader understanding of your full story, you have the confidence to share Jesus with a world desperate for the very thing you have—an entirely new identity.

Don't Miss It

- If we don't know who we are, it's really hard to show the world who Jesus is.
- From Genesis to Revelation the Bible tells one story—ours. We are loved, chosen, forgiven, and called for His purposes.
- Identity isn't dictated by behavior (which is good news for anyone who's ever lost it in the Costco parking lot).
- Your adoption in Christ is permanent, your acceptance is unshakable, and His faithfulness is forever.

Chapter 6

Bad Blood and Broken Windows

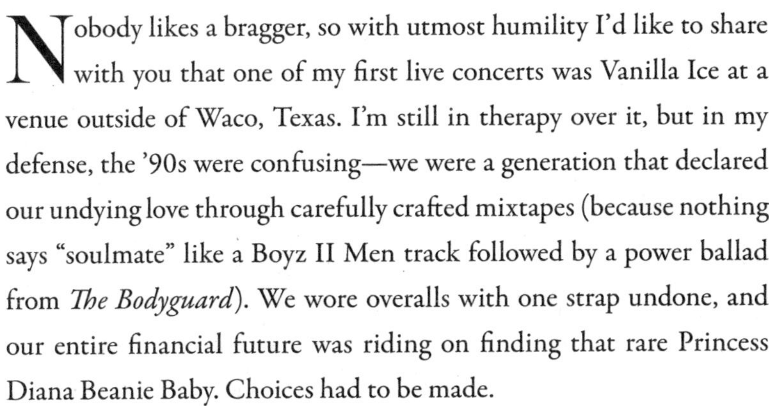

Nobody likes a bragger, so with utmost humility I'd like to share with you that one of my first live concerts was Vanilla Ice at a venue outside of Waco, Texas. I'm still in therapy over it, but in my defense, the '90s were confusing—we were a generation that declared our undying love through carefully crafted mixtapes (because nothing says "soulmate" like a Boyz II Men track followed by a power ballad from *The Bodyguard*). We wore overalls with one strap undone, and our entire financial future was riding on finding that rare Princess Diana Beanie Baby. Choices had to be made.

So when my daughter, Kate, asked for Taylor Swift tickets as her first concert, it was an immediate "heck yes," even if it cost me a few Beanie Babies to get her there. Now whether you adore Taylor Swift or you're just mildly confused by the whole friendship-bracelet situation, there's no denying that she has basically taken over the world. She's the most-awarded artist in American Music Awards history, has fourteen Grammys (including *four* for Album of the Year), and somehow managed to break Ticketmaster when Eras Tour tickets went on sale. If dominance were a person, it would be wearing bright red lipstick and a Travis Kelce jersey.

Now we all know that nobody wins when we play the comparison game—but seeing all of T-Swizzle's success gave me a little moxie to check my own rankings. So I clicked right on over to the Apple podcast charts to see how my podcasts are currently stacking up and, I wish I were kidding, but at this very moment I'm getting beat out by *The Cat in the Hat* podcast. And if that's not humbling enough, I'm also losing to a podcast called *12 Hour Sound Machines*. Yes, you read that right. A *no loop, no fade* sound machine podcast—just white noise—is ranking higher than me. So basically, there's a large group of people (in addition to my teens) who would prefer listening to *nothing* more than my actual words.

That brings me to a question that feels excruciatingly pressing at the moment: What's Taylor Swift's secret to success? Experts say it's the perfect mix of brilliant songwriting, personal branding, and business acumen. Harvard has literally studied her marketing genius, and Berklee College of Music analyzed her songs and declared their popularity is because they are "instantly relatable."[1] Are you getting this? She has a level of success that virtually no one can relate to, yet the very thing that makes her music so popular is its "relatability."

Clearly I can't say I relate to every detail of Taylor Swift's life (and I doubt she had the privilege of seeing Vanilla Ice like myself), but I can relate to one thing: conflict. Specifically, that full-blown feud she had with Katy Perry awhile back. I'm thankful my conflicts aren't headline-worthy, but let's be honest, who among us hasn't had a "Katy Perry" in our life? Maybe yours didn't steal your backup dancers (which, hilariously, was the crux of the conflict), but we've all watched a friendship unravel over something small that somehow spiraled into something big.

Taylor's response to the Katy Perry feud was a tad more epic than mine—I usually just vent to my husband or send a passive-aggressive text that I immediately regret. But Taylor jumped out there with the full genius move, writing her Grammy-nominated smash hit, "Bad Blood."

But stay with me, because *this is getting good now* (yes, I'm unapologetically inserting TS lyrics now). Years into the big feud, in an unexpected not-so-mean-girl move, Katy Perry sent Taylor an *actual* olive branch before one of Taylor's concerts with a note that basically said, "My bad." Obviously, *Band-Aids don't fix bullet holes*, but years of pettiness and pointed lyrics were squashed with this one kind and humble move. Gosh—I wish all the conflict in our lives could be instantly resolved as simply as sending an olive branch to a friend's dressing room before a sold-out show.

Would I be jumping out on a limb to say we might be living in the most offendable culture of all time? To be fair, I've never experienced another culture, but in a world where people are offended by the design of a Starbucks holiday cup, and the mention of a political preference on social media causes people to use their powerful "unfollow" button—the "problems" we lose sleep over are getting a little silly. Come to think of it, maybe that's why the sound machine podcast is so popular.

I wish I could say that, as Christians, we're less offendable—but then I think back to the great church worship wars of the '90s: hymns versus Hillsong. Not to mention (which I'm totally mentioning) how easily we're drawn offsides by Bible translations, the carpet color in the sanctuary, and the near spiritual crisis that was brewing when coffee made its way into church services. I heard a pastor once say it's funny how offended we are as Christians, considering our entire faith is based on a person who died for our own personal offenses.[2] Ouch.

Relationships > Religious Activities.
That's the word from Jesus.

Jesus cares how we handle conflict, so much so that it's addressed directly in Matthew 5. He says, if you're heading to the altar and remember someone has an issue with you—don't finish your latte, don't check your phone, don't comment on the pastor's skinny jeans—just drop everything and go make things right with that person.

For what it's worth, if I wrote the rules, there'd be a little more stewing time allotted in Jesus' approach. Maybe a girls' night out to rehash the issue, a good old pros-and-cons list, or at least a let's-give-them-time-to-apologize-first waiting period. But nope—Jesus essentially says, "Stop everything; don't pass Go; head directly to reconciliation." When He tells us to *leave it at the altar* (see v. 24), He's specifically referencing those times when we think we're too busy doing religious things to go take care of business. (Makes me wonder if He's referencing the times at church when I'm belting out, "My chains are gone, I've been set free," while also giving my spouse the death glare across the pew after last night's "discussion.")

This one's easy to miss, but Relationships > Religious Activities. That's the word from Jesus.

Am I the only one who finds it interesting how we want grace for our mistakes and justice for everyone else's? We want forgiveness freely given when we mess up, but we're pretty tight with it when someone else wrongs us.

This is the heart issue Jesus cares about. Yes, He wants reconciliation for us, but more than that, He wants restoration. He knows that when we leave conflict unresolved, it's igniting a tiny spark today that holds full dumpster-fire potential for tomorrow.

The Glass-Repair Gospel

I first heard about the "broken windows" theory a few years ago from one of Brett's high school football coaches who, like most Texas football coaches, loves full-contact tackling drills in August second only to Jesus.

The "broken windows" theory basically says that if you ignore the little stuff—like shattered windows, graffiti, or that neighbor who thinks their front yard is landfill—then bigger problems aren't far behind. Why? Because if it *looks* like no one cares, people act like no one cares.

Neglect sends a message: If no one's fixing the broken stuff, it only gets worse.

Picture this: Two buildings, both have a broken window. The first one gets fixed fast—nice, clean glass, back in business. The second one is left shattered for weeks, and before you know it, the local hoodlums have moved in, started a bonfire in the breakroom, and are selling questionable gummies out of the second floor. What started as a cracked window ends with Keith Morrison narrating the final scene.

Now there's a lot of debate and criticism on how this theory impacts police practices and criminology, but it's a good word on handling conflict. Neglect sends a message: If no one's fixing the broken stuff, it only gets worse.

If Jesus used the broken windows analogy, He'd probably say that the moment conflict shows up in a relationship—and it will—don't hang around. File the insurance claim and get the glass guy out there ASAP. Because when conflict starts creeping in—hurt feelings, sharp words, icy silence—that's the critical time to show up, name it, apologize for it, and fix it. Otherwise, cracked windows turn into crack houses (I apologize, that felt too dramatic).

Said more diplomatically, the longer we ignore conflict, the messier it gets. But honestly, we don't need a criminology theory to tell us that. We've all lived it. Broken trust, tense dinners, and that one group text you stopped replying to—they don't just magically fix themselves. They grow until one day there's a full-blown *Dateline* episode with your neighbors on camera saying, "I had no idea; she always seemed so nice."

Fenced In

When I was a kid, I remember my grandfather had an *issue* with his neighbor—one of those classic, long-standing, old-man disputes where no one could quite remember what started it, but neither party was backing down. If you asked my grandfather what "Old Man Heinzman" had done, he'd give you a vague answer about how Heinzman was not to be trusted. My grandfather was *certain* the man was out to get him—probably even plotting to steal from him. And so, for years, he kept a close watch, peeking through the blinds, grumbling about Heinzman under his breath, just waiting for some heinous act that was sure to come.

One day at lunchtime my dad pulled into my grandparents' driveway. A contractor was there taking measurements and casually mentioned to my dad that my grandfather had hired him to put up a chain-link fence. Naturally, my dad went to my grandfather for an explanation, and, without hesitation, he resolutely said it was to keep Old Man Heinzman off his property. (By the way, we're talking a chain-link fence in his perfectly cute little residential neighborhood.)

My dad was over it at this point. So in an effort to de-escalate the situation and address the not-so-neighborly conflict head-on, he went on a mission to find Old Man Heinzman so the two of them could get this silliness worked out once and for all. That's when the whole situation took a rather ironic turn—my dad soon learned that Old Man Heinzman had been dead for years.

Building fences for long-passed grievances isn't unique to my grandfather. It's the perfect picture of the offenses we hold on to; typically, in the name of standing our ground, protecting our reputation, or proving we're right. Part of the problem is that we've forgotten who the real enemy is. Scripture is crystal clear: Satan comes to steal, kill, and destroy—but we forget that one of his most effective weapons is division. Jesus warns us that a "house divided against itself will not stand" (Matt. 12:25 NKJV). So when we allow ourselves to remain upset, insulted, and offended, we're unknowingly playing right into the enemy's hand.

It would be much easier if the enemy's agenda was obvious, instead of the slow, steady drip of small offenses that build with thoughts like:

- *I can't believe she didn't say hello.*
- *She thinks her kids are so amazing.*
- *Of course we weren't invited.*
- *Clearly she's trying to prove a point.*

These often insignificant slights seep deep into our hearts, corroding friendships, marriages, and ministries—one section of chain-link fence at a time.

Jesus came to give us complete freedom—yet when we hold on to grudges, stay offended, and refuse to reconcile, we willingly step back into the very bondage He's already broken. That's why Jesus is so serious about it. And, similarly, that's why the enemy is so serious about it. As Lewis Smedes so beautifully put it: "To forgive is to set a prisoner free and discover that the prisoner was you."[3]

My grandfather's fence was meant to keep his enemy out, but in reality he was the one being trapped inside. Theologian Warren Wiersbe says it bluntly: "We put ourselves into a terrible prison when we refuse to be reconciled."[4] And that prison? Well, it looks a lot like an unsightly chain-link fence built on the foundation of small offenses that go unaddressed in the moment the conflict arises.

Don't miss it: When it comes to conflict, the real question isn't "Who should we keep out?" it's "Why are we fencing ourselves in?"

Hot Cross Buns and Other Ways We Suffer

To date, I have never served time in prison. But if I do one day, it's either because my husband won't stop blasting Queen in the car, or I finally lost it at the elementary school recorder concert featuring "Hot Cross Buns." Yet I've repeatedly imprisoned myself by building fences intended to keep someone else out. At the risk of getting too personal, here's one of my more unflattering examples.

I had a falling out with a friend I've known for several decades. For reasons I'm not sure of but still regret, I did not go to this friend and address the tension head-on. I made some assumptions. I got offended. And what started as a singular broken window became all-out vandalism in a matter of months. To further complicate the situation, our lives intersected enough that there was no pretending we were fine. We passed each other daily while we were driving, exercising, or just doing life.

Over time, my grandfather's chain-link fence didn't seem so preposterous once I began constructing my own. Then, something unexpected happened. Her family got involved with foster care, something that's obviously close to my heart and tied to JB's past. When my husband and I heard they received their first placement, we jumped in to help. And somewhere between digging out our old pack and play and buying newborn diapers, my heart began to shift.

I was at her house one evening when she did something incredibly kind: she stopped mid-diaper change and said, "I'm sorry." She acknowledged the distance in our relationship and expressed the regret she had for not being present during our foster care journey. She did what I should have done years ago—repaired the window.

There was no rehashing the past, assigning fault, or even exchanging olive branches. But with two simple words, "I'm sorry," healing took root.

This is just one of many situations where I wish I had let things go long ago—dismantling the self-righteous fence posts I've been cementing with every small offense. I wish I would have been the person before the apology that I am now that the apology has been offered.

Here's one last thing about reconciliation: Mission always trumps misunderstanding. In other words, when we're busy doing the hard work of living out our faith—whether it's caring for orphans, providing a meal, or raising our kids to know Jesus—there's simply no time for fence building, only window repairing.

Conflict is inevitable. Someone will wrong us. Someone will misunderstand us. Someone will take something from us—maybe our peace, our reputation, our spotlight. If we're not careful, our biggest victories will be tainted by the battles we refuse to let go. That's why conflict resolution matters. It's not just about keeping the peace; it's about keeping our freedom. Yes, there will be some places where we need boundaries in relationships that are beyond repair. That's not what we're talking about here. It's the petty grievances that steal our joy and freedom.

Who's your Katy Perry?

Whether you owe the apology or deserve one, she's not the enemy; there is a real one, and his weapon of choice is division. So let's follow Jesus' instruction and drop whatever we're holding, leave it at the altar, and make the first move like our freedom depends on it. Because it probably does.

Don't Miss It

- It's interesting how we want grace for our mistakes and justice for everyone else's.
- When we remain upset, insulted, and offended, we're unknowingly playing right into the enemy's hand.
- It's never too late to tear down fences and live in freedom.

Chapter 7

From C-Sections to Cherry Bombs: The Memoirs of Parenthood

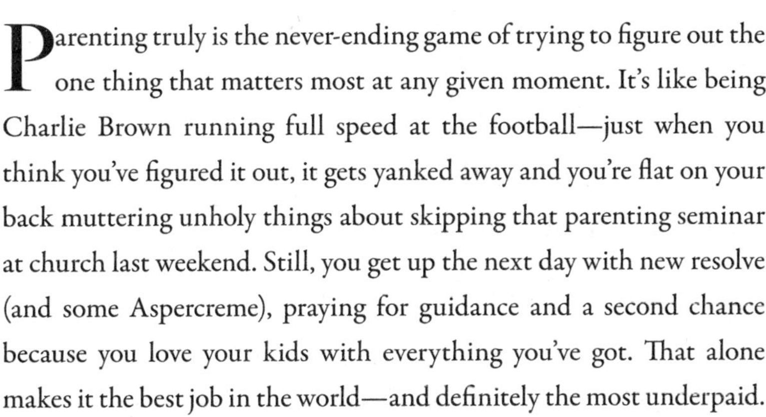

Parenting truly is the never-ending game of trying to figure out the one thing that matters most at any given moment. It's like being Charlie Brown running full speed at the football—just when you think you've figured it out, it gets yanked away and you're flat on your back muttering unholy things about skipping that parenting seminar at church last weekend. Still, you get up the next day with new resolve (and some Aspercreme), praying for guidance and a second chance because you love your kids with everything you've got. That alone makes it the best job in the world—and definitely the most underpaid.

Somewhere around age fifty, I finally got a minute to sit down, grab a Diet Dr Pepper, and reflect on the sheer joy—and absolute chaos—of raising kids. It's that sweet spot where you're past the playdate and carpool phase but not quite at the point where you start calling your dog Bubba and ordering sweaters for him off Amazon. You've graduated to parenting "young adults" who have no money, no job, and all the answers. And you finally have time to analyze some of the mishaps—like when your teenage son asked for a Cherry Bomb exhaust and you said yes, thinking it was a Slurpee flavor, and now he blows the whole neighborhood out of their beds every time he fires up his truck for an early morning trip to the gym. Or maybe that's just us.

Mike and I aren't your typical fifty-somethings when it comes to parenting—we've got a second grader. Which means I'm over here managing menopause and math facts. Flash cards and hot flashes were never meant to coexist—that's my truth. The good news? We've settled into a more relaxed version of parenting. The bad news? Our eight-year-old recently asked the baseball coach for "Hells Bells" as his walk-up song. So then we were left explaining that he has older siblings—who are clearly troubled—and that we really want to stay on the team, and we promise he's not *that* kid (while secretly wondering if he is, in fact, *that* kid).

Pink Journal Parenting

Recently, I found a little pink journal my mom gave me on my first Mother's Day, twenty-two years ago. Inside was a sweet inscription: "To Cynthia on your first Mother's Day: A book to journal your days with Kate."

Always the achiever, I took my new journaling role seriously. On June 27, 2003—two months into parenting—I wrote my first entry. It was a deep, overly detailed dive into everything: Kate's unplanned C-section, my pre-eclampsia, and her eating, sleeping, and pooping habits. I noted how she looked just like her dad (a bit disappointing since I did most of the work) and confessed that the first two months had been a marginal disaster. Mostly because she had her days and nights reversed and I was surviving on fourteen minutes of sleep per week. I was exhausted, frustrated, and living proof that mastitis is no joke. Yet with a hint of optimism, I noted we were "just now beginning to see the light at the end of the tunnel."

Oh, bless it—sweet, naive new mom. If I could go back and write a note to myself in that journal, it would say: *Girl, that's not the light at the end of the tunnel. That's the fridge light you left on at 2:00 a.m. while crying over a gallon of Blue Bell Cookie Two Step. The real tunnel is long and dark, and when you finally army crawl out the other side, you'll need Botox, a tummy tuck, and earplugs to wear in your driveway just in case your son remote-starts his truck from his bedroom.*

Still, I worked really hard at solving new-mom dilemmas back then and quickly discovered that mothering doesn't come naturally to everyone. True story: At one of our first pediatrician visits, I asked the doctor how to know when it's time to size up in diapers. Are you following me? I looked a board-certified medical professional—someone who attended twenty-plus years of schooling to fulfill their noble calling to help small humans live healthy and productive lives—in the eye and asked: Can you break it down for me how to know when my child's Huggies are too tight?

That was the first and last pediatrician visit Mike attended with me. Turns out, you can earn degrees in just about everything except common sense. And decades later, I'm still worrying about diapers—wondering if I'll need them myself before our youngest finishes high school.

In those early parenting years, the stakes feel impossibly high. You're sterilizing bottles like it's surgery prep, having your car seat installation double-checked at the fire station, and googling whether crib sleep habits correlate with college insomnia. You're exhausted but determined, desperate to get it right—but painfully unsure what *right* even looks like.

If I could whisper one thing to my pink-journaling self, it would be this: *What feels most important in the moment usually isn't. I know you're second-guessing everything and assuming the mom next to you has it all figured out. But parenting is full of unknowns. There's no single formula for doing it right. There are high highs, low lows, and lots of sacred, ordinary moments in between. So throw in a Baby Einstein video, pray with everything you've got, give yourself some grace, and be brave as you size up those diapers.*

It Was Never about the Game Anyway

Let's just say there was a time when I sat in courtrooms dealing with high-stakes legal cases. I settled six-figure demands with the full authority of a Fortune 500 company. I interpreted contracts with major business implications (lucky for me, I took contracts twice—said no one ever).

But nothing compares to the pressure of being snack mom during T-ball season.

One innocent "yes" and suddenly I'm locked into six weeks of anxiety, color-coded reminders, and a low-grade fear I'll forget which Saturday is mine and crush the dreams of a dozen orange-slice-deprived six-year-olds. I've parented for a long time, and while most things have stayed consistent, snacks have not. The ethics behind a bag of Goldfish are a minefield. Are there GMCs? Or is it GNCs? Maybe HFCs? It needs to be gluten-free, nut-free, dye-free, cage-free—and ideally joy-free, since fun has apparently been banned from childhood nutrition.

Looking back, however, preschool snacks were the gateway drug to our family's sports addiction. When I married a college athlete, I apparently signed up for a sports regimen with the intensity most people reserve for disarming a nuclear weapon. Our kids have collectively played everything: softball, baseball, tennis, football, lacrosse, volleyball, basketball, soccer, dodgeball, and, most recently, pickleball.

We've woken up at dawn for Saturday morning tournaments, stayed out too late for Sunday night championships, sweated through August doubleheaders, frozen on metal bleachers, endured deafening gymnasiums—and once, I even attended a baseball game while fighting a stomach bug. It ended badly for everyone involved. We've paid for uniforms, league fees, private lessons, new cleats, team dinners—and yes, we've brought the snacks.

Why? Because sports are woven into the fabric of our family.

Along the way, I'd occasionally run into some ancient mom (who, turns out, was my current age) who'd say, "Savor every moment—it goes by fast." I'd nod politely while thinking, *Okay, Karen, but I'm snack mom today so let's move it along.*

But eventually—just as Karen warned—the end comes.

A few nights ago, I sat in the stands one last time, lights humming, gripping my son's Fathead as the innings ticked down on his final baseball game. I took pictures. I held back tears. I tried to process that it was over. The season I hoped would never end—finally did.

And now I can see it: The real value—the eternal stuff—was never in the tournament brackets or stats. It lived in the in-between moments. The sideline talks, the car rides home, the quiet character-building no one tracked on GameChanger or posted on Instagram. Here's the truth:

> Brett won't remember how many times I scrubbed dirt from his white baseball pants,
>
> > But he'll remember my words after he was benched in a key game.
>
> He won't remember how tryouts went for his first select team,
>
> > But he'll remember Mike's kindness toward the kid who "got his spot."
>
> He won't remember where they placed in district freshman year,
>
> > But he'll remember the funeral his team attended to support one of their own.

He won't remember his ERA or strikeout count his junior year,
  But he'll remember our talks about humility and respecting his coach.

He won't remember the batting order, the bracket, or the stats,
  But he'll remember the grit it took to come back after a devastating pitching injury.

Don't miss it: The lessons far outlive the game.

Whether it's the heartbreak of not making varsity, the nerves before the curtain rises, or the sting of a B- in pre-calc after studying all night—these are the very moments that can shape our kids to look more like Jesus. Humility. Empathy. Compassion. Learning to cheer for others, even when it comes at their own expense.

The real value—the eternal stuff—was never in the tournament brackets or stats. It lived in the in-between moments.

Yet parenting holds a painful tension: knowing that character is built in the face of disappointment and godly success is rarely measured by applause, while also wanting desperately to clean up their messes and make their road easier.

Take it from me: The day will come when the cleats will be packed away, the glove will be sitting on a bookcase, and the trophies will be collecting dust in the attic—and what will remain is the person our kid has become after the last proverbial pitch has been thrown.

That's why we keep choosing the parenting road less traveled, whispering reminders to ourselves that what feels urgent today isn't what matters most in the end. We anchor ourselves in what lasts longer than trophies, titles, and college acceptances, saying ...

> Give me a coach who is building my son into a man of integrity any day ...
>
> over a coach who knows how to assemble a winning team.
>
> Give me the late bloomer, awkward young athlete who sits on the bench any day ...
>
> over a kid who is arrogant, entitled, and disrespectful to the adults on the field.
>
> Give me a parent who is late to practices and forgets the snacks any day ...
>
> over one who barks, belittles, and behaves badly in front of my kids.
>
> Give me a kid who knows their value is not tied to their performance any day ...
>
> over a prospective D1 college athlete.

Give me a Friday night at home when my junior high daughter wasn't invited to "the cool girls' sleepover" any day ...

over an invitation that includes drama and gossip, and excludes others.

Give me a girl who didn't get asked to prom any day ...

over one who is materialistic, compromising, and desperate to get a boy's attention.

Give me a son who doesn't receive an academic award any day ...

over a kid who is stressed out, strung out, and convinced their worth is tied to a test score.

Give me a teen who loses his student council race any day ...

over a kid whose charisma and class rank trumps his character.

Give me a senior who doesn't get into their dream school while quietly trusting God has a different path for them any day ...

over a kid who can't celebrate a friend's success.

Give me a young adult who has to pivot with grace and pray through disappointment any day ...

over the one who loses sight of *whose* they are.

The Long Game of Parenting

As much as I believe that the little things often turn out to be the big things in parenting—and the things that seem most important in the moment are typically not—I also know this: we all get it wrong sometimes. I could write an entire book just on the times I've missed it (oh, just did) and my kids would happily write the foreword, probably in all caps.

The truth is, there are no guarantees in parenting. We can pour out our hearts, pray relentlessly, show up every single day—and still watch our kids take paths we never imagined or hoped for. Even so, the best parenting advice I ever received was to picture what I want my kids to be at twenty-five and then consider what I can do today to help them get there. That philosophy has reshaped my parenting, reminding me that the little choices we make each day matter.

We keep choosing the parenting road less traveled, whispering reminders to ourselves that what feels urgent today isn't what matters most in the end.

Kate graduated from college recently, and in a rare moment of maturity (mine, not hers), I asked her what we got right as parents—and what we didn't. She started by gently pointing out that we didn't always let them see the hard stuff, like financial stress, the normal life struggles, and even the moments that made our faith shaky. But then she went on to say that what we did best was constantly reminding them that *character counts twice*. In other words, you can get everything else right, but if your character is compromised, none of it really matters.

"Character counts twice" has been a quiet anthem of our parenting all these years (along with kindness, doing the hard things, and pursuing Jesus with everything we've got). I suppose that's the one redeeming part of all those Charlie Brown moments in parenting—when you've been knocked flat on your back, you have a great view to figure out who you hope your kids become when they are twenty-five and what you're doing (or not doing) now to get them there.

Because anyone who's been journaling longer than the first panicked pediatrician visit knows the "character counts twice" moments are hard-won, usually somewhere between the "Hells Bells" and Cherry Bomb–exhaust dumpster fires. And that's why we trust God, who, in His infinite kindness, keeps gently reminding us that the things that feel most important in the moment—grades, friendships, college résumés, and yes, even sports—rarely are.

Don't Miss It

- A parenting truth: What feels most important almost never is. (Unless it's lice. Then panic.)
- The real wins aren't in the scores or trophies but in the character that's built on the sidelines.
- Sometimes the road to character includes "Hells Bells" and a noise complaint from the neighbors.

My Journal Entry: Twenty Years Later

Hey there, thought I'd check back in. Turns out a lot can happen in twenty years. I started this journal with the best of intentions, back when the biggest decisions were about diaper sizes (which was a real mind-boggler, BTW) and wondering if anyone in the house would ever sleep again. There's so much I could say about life since then, but instead I'll just share a few things I wish I would have known:

1. Do yourself a favor and start brushing up on acronym-speak now, while the kids are still in Velcro shoes and think you're brilliant. Because one day you will hand them a cell phone, pay the bill for said phone, and they'll start texting things like "IDC," "IMO," and "LMK if it slaps." And you'll be googling "slaps" to see if they need counseling while also learning TTYL means "talk to you later," not "totally take your laxative."
2. One day your teenage son will walk right past the perfectly good coffee pot in your kitchen and head out into a torrential downpour to hit a drive-thru for caffeine. He'll toss out a quick "BRB" (be right back)—and assure you not to worry because "safety's my middle name." And you'll believe him. Don't. He's lying. He's about to total his truck. It won't be his fault, but it will be the most expensive $10 IAC (Iced Americano) you'll ever buy.

3. What starts with a family bike ride—just the four of you—will get a little weird when you feel a repeated nudge that someone's missing. That's God about to launch you into the wildest, holiest, and on-your-knees-praying adventure of your life: foster care and adoption. It'll be beautiful and brutal and 100 percent worth it. You'll cry in Target (center section by the baby onesies), and even your closest friends will wonder what you got yourself into. Eventually, it'll bring you the cutest, curly-headed chaos machine you've ever met—and you'll have learned that hard and holy often walk hand in hand. And one day in your fifties, you'll find yourself balancing zoo field trips and osteoporosis while also using weird texting lingo like "bet" (i.e., "sure") when your new thirty-something mom friends want to come over and play Mahjong.
4. You'll take your daughter to football games at your beloved private Christian alma mater from the time she's a baby, convinced—FRFR (for real, for real)—that she'll follow in your holy footsteps for college. Spoiler alert: she won't. Instead, she'll choose a massive public university where she'll see things that make your prayer life more consistent and your eye twitch more permanent. But you'll watch her grow into her own faith, learn to love people really well, and start serving the least of these. And one day, she'll become one of your

very best friends—hilarious, loved by all, fluent in sarcasm—and you'll wonder how someone that cool ever came from your gene pool.

I could go on forever with these pink-journal parenting thoughts, but more than anything, please know that you've shown up when it wasn't easy, loved when it felt impossible, and believed in your kids' future even when the obstacles looked insurmountable.

You've found a work-life rhythm that's not just good for your family but right for you and your calling. You've loved their dad well—and tried harder when you missed the mark. You've surrounded yourself with friends who are kind, grounded, and chase after what really matters.

And twenty years later, I'm happy to report: the kids are turning out just fine. They love you. They love Mike. They love Jesus. They're kind and humble. (Sure, they still make the occasional knucklehead move, and yes, you'll still want to wring a neck now and then.)

If history repeats itself, I probably won't crack open this pink journal again until I'm in my seventies—BMH (bless my heart). So for now, be kind to yourself. Trust that you're getting more right than wrong. Take it from me (and the older moms who seem irrelevant right now), on the days that feel impossibly long—they are actually deceptively short.

Chapter 8

Being a Generous Dorcas

I read about a man flying from Baltimore to Los Angeles for business.[1] His sister, a former flight attendant, was nearing the end of her battle with pancreatic cancer. Distraught, yet determined to honor her legacy, he approached a flight attendant with a simple request: he wanted an extra set of those plastic wings. His sister never had the chance to take her final flight, so he was searching for ways to honor her however he could.

The flight attendant, upon hearing his story, revealed that she actually knew his sister. Without hesitation, she offered him the extra wings. After the plane took off, the flight attendant went even further for the man with the terminally ill sister. She handed him the intercom mic and gave him the chance to share his sister's story with everyone on board.

Before I go any further, I must share a few rogue thoughts relating to air travel that in no way relate to this story:

1. There's no such thing as an atheist during turbulence. Who's with me? When the pilot turns on the seat-belt sign mid-flight, surely I'm not the only one who immediately scans the cabin for confirmation that we should go ahead and put our head between our knees—only to find flight attendants casually handing out snacks while everyone else naps?
2. Has anyone noticed that the preflight protocol is grossly out of touch with today's modern air travel? Let's stop kidding ourselves about inflating that life vest by mouth; I was out of breath tying my shoes at security. Instead, can we please focus on more pressing matters with an updated preflight spiel that goes more like this:
   - Just because you were TSA Pre doesn't mean you're better than everyone else—you just waited longer at the gate for the rest of us, so let's dial down the smugness.
   - If you can't figure out how to work the seat-belt, that's on you. But you know what else is on you? Your shoes. They are not optional and must stay on your feet for the entire duration of a domestic flight. (Yes, I'm including you flip-flops, Crocs, and Birkenstocks.)

- Put your cell phone on airplane mode, don't smoke, don't block the bathroom, blah, blah, blah. Truly we'd rather you vape, blast Metallica without headphones, or spend the better part of an hour talking about your Aunt Martha's cat—but for the love of all things good, do *not* crack open a tuna sandwich at 30,000 feet. (Ditto for egg salad, hard boiled eggs, and beef jerky.) A little common sense goes a long way when it comes to flight-friendly foods.
- Final note: Your seatmate's quarterly sales projections are not your business. Neither is the spicy rom-com that 12B is watching like it's date night. Eyes forward; Kindle up. Everyone wins when we mind our own business.

3. Last thing: As a lifelong Christian I know that Jesus is supposed to be our copilot. But when it comes to air travel, would it be frowned upon to also request Sully Sullenberger just in case? Asking for a friend.

Okay, back to my pre-rant story.

The man was so grateful for the opportunity to talk about his sister that he started sharing stories about their childhood, her children, the impact she'd had on so many lives while flying, and now, the painful reality of her final days. He even passed his phone around the plane, letting passengers see pictures of her and asking if anyone would be willing to write her a note of encouragement. More than ninety people responded with drawings and letters. There was even an item quilted by one passenger, and another person made an origami flower arrangement from cocktail napkins. (Presumably all done with their shoes on and sans tuna.)

One especially touching note said this: "Your brother made me love you, and I don't even know you."[2]

Here's a truth that's easy to miss: Every time we offer kind words, stand in the gap, show up, speak up, or even know when to shut up, we're painting a picture of our Savior. Our actions help people see Jesus in a way that makes them love Him—even if they've never met Him.

Threefold Generosity

If you're anything like me, when you hear the word *generosity*—especially in a faith context—you immediately clutch your purse and think of money. It's one of those things we throw into the bucket of "topics preachers talk about twice a year," typically when the church is over budget. And yes, financial generosity matters. But if we think finances are the whole story (or even the majority of the story) on living generously, we've missed the bigger picture. The thing about generosity is that typically it's not loud and labeled; it looks more like availability, compassion, and—like the story above—sometimes even origami. Here are a few examples of generosity that have marked my own life.

After one of the most painful setbacks I've faced in Christian ministry—one marked by deep church hurt and multiple layers of misunderstanding—I was crushed. I was defeated. I had stepped into that new role with full confidence that it was from the Lord, mainly because it was something I never would have pursued on my own. The call had come completely out of the blue, and after much prayer, I said yes. It was like nothing I had experienced—using new giftings, seeing kingdom impact, and working harder than ever, while also balancing the needs of my family during the early months of COVID quarantine. And then just as quickly as it started, the opportunity ended with little explanation. I was left questioning the motives of the people I had long respected and confided in—while also questioning God.

At the same time, my husband's law firm was going through an unexpected transition, and his income had taken a significant hit. Not to mention mine had just been eliminated. And yet, as only God can do, I felt Him nudging me to start a new podcast and speaking ministry. I was painfully honest letting the Lord know I was licking some wounds from the last time I gave Him a yes, and I was pretty sure I wasn't cut out for Christian ministry. Not to mention the timing felt absurd. Spiritually, I was raw. Financially, I felt depleted. (Which is actually God's preferred timing, now that I think about it.)

I called my mom and asked her to pray—and if Dorothy prays for it and you don't get it, then you probably don't need it. A few hours later, she told me to stop by on my way to pick up the kids from school. When I arrived, she and my dad handed me an envelope. They looked me in the eyes and told me how much they believed in me—or, better yet, how much they believed in God *through* me.

Inside was a sizeable check to start my next chapter of ministry. Now here's the truth—I never cashed it. What mattered most in that moment wasn't the financial support; it was their belief in me when I couldn't see past the disillusionment. Their generosity wasn't about funding a ministry but reminding me that I still had one.

A close friend and I took our kids to Cicis Pizza many years ago. I know, sorry to brag about my fanciness, but I'm #blessed that way. While our kids were busy touching every surface and contracting Ebola, my friend confided in me, tearfully, about one of her children who was struggling both academically and socially. She admitted that everything just seemed harder for him than for other kids his age, leaving her anxious about his future.

Not long after our conversation ended, a large, rather imposing man approached her. He pointed toward the buffet line full of kids and asked if one of the boys was hers. My friend looked where he was pointing—right at the son she had just been talking about—and said, "Yes, he's mine."

Then, in a quiet but intentional voice, the man said, "I know this is going to sound strange, but the Lord drew my attention to your son and told me to assure you that he is going to be a great leader one day."

And with that, he turned and walked away. He didn't offer money or a solution, just a sentence. His words of hope, delivered in obedience, became a part of someone else's story—words he likely has no idea are still being held on to today.

Generosity is rarely loud and labeled; it looks more like availability, compassion, and standing in the gap for others.

I cried after I dropped off JB at school one morning.

For most parents, it was just another chaotic kindergarten day—backpacks, lunches, and convincing a five-year-old that he is not *actually* Patrick Mahomes and required to wear his jersey every day. But for me, I had been dreading this day for weeks. The kindergarten class was going on a field trip. I had wrestled with the idea of keeping JB home, but his excitement was so palpable that I couldn't bring myself to ruin it for him.

It had been only a short time since the isolation of COVID, and JB was still struggling with appropriate school behavior some days. The impulsivity that was sometimes hard to manage in the classroom weighed heavily on my heart. Only the room moms were allowed to chaperone, which filled me with anxiety. I remember praying desperately, asking God to be with JB, to guide the staff, and to give the room mom an extra measure of patience and grace. I also confessed my pride—how I feared judgment from others based on my son's behavior and my parenting.

As I sat at home that morning, filled with worry, I started receiving text messages from the mom assigned to JB's group—someone I didn't even know, who went out of her way to get my cell number. She sent pictures of JB and told me how well he was doing. Throughout the day, she kept me updated, even going so far as to wait after school, to give me and JB both a hug and share how he had stolen her heart that day at the zoo.

A Theology of Generosity

Whether it's believing in someone, speaking encouragement into their most vulnerable places, or offering grace when it's least expected—that's a picture of living generously. Throughout the New Testament, Jesus speaks of generosity, but rarely did He make it about money. It's a powerful reminder that true generosity has far more to do with our hearts than our finances. These stories above, along with so many others I've witnessed over the years, have taught me this about the theology of generosity:

> Generous people give far more than just their money.
> Generous people step in when others step back.
> Generous people obey God's prompting even when it's uncomfortable.
> Generous people know their words hold more power than their finances.
> Generous people instinctively stand in the gap of others' struggles.
> Generous people reject the scarcity mindset and trust in God's limitless provision.
> Generous people know that selflessness sets apart their faith.

Bad Name, Good Point

The New Testament tells the story of a woman named Dorcas (moment of silence, please, for her name) which means "gazelle." Interestingly, she also had the Aramaic name Tabitha, which—plot twist—means the exact same thing: "gazelle." So basically, if you're a gazelle either way, I'd like to recommend we join forces in suggesting she lean into the name Tabitha ten out of ten times because nobody wants to be a Dorcas. But since this has nothing to do with generosity I'll move on, reluctantly.

Dorcas was a culturally successful businesswoman. She was known to be full of good works and charitable acts. She took care of the widows. She sewed clothes for those in need. She wasn't just *thinking* about doing good; her days were spent *actually doing* good. At some point, she became sick and died. Those surrounding her were understandably devastated. They begged Peter to come to their town for a last-minute Hail Mary to try to revive her. When Peter got to the place where she lay dead, he found her surrounded by heartbroken widows who were weeping and holding up their "tunics and garments" as evidence of Dorcas's generosity and kindness (Acts 9:39). Then, through the power of Jesus, Peter raised her from the dead.

I'm praying none of us has a near-death experience as dramatic as Dorcas's, but her story gives us a few thoughts on what generosity really looks like:

Lying on our deathbed, who will be surrounding us? Our family? Naturally. Close friends? Hopefully. But would our room be filled with people so impacted by our generosity that they are pleading with doctors, ministers, or even prophets to save our lives? Would there be people testifying how they fell in love with Jesus when they didn't even know Him because of how we served? Would our smallest acts of generosity be someone else's greatest testimony?

Don't miss this: In Dorcas's moment of crisis, the widows held up the clothes on their backs as proof of how she lived. There's not one discussion of the wealth she had accumulated, only that which she had gifted. What would be the evidence of our generosity? Would people hold up clothes donated, notes written, meals provided, finances given, kind words spoken in defense of our generosity? Or would it tell a different story, one of good intentions overshadowed by hurriedness and missed opportunities?

Generous people reject the scarcity mindset and trust in God's limitless provision.

We are all called to be a Dorcas (so to speak)—which means, bottom line, the seemingly small things matter, like loving rambunctious kids or speaking God's truth to a mom at the pizza buffet. These little moment-by-moment acts have long-lasting impact on those we help while also transforming us in the process.

That's not all (said like an informercial). Yes, generosity is good for us spiritually—but it turns out, it's also good for us physically. Studies show that people who live generously tend to have lower blood pressure, stronger immune systems, higher energy, and reduced risk of depression.[3] As if that weren't enough, generosity also does a number on anxiety. The simple act of giving actually calms the brain—literally. It releases chemicals that quiet the amygdala, the part of your brain that sounds the stress alarm. Turns out, showing up for someone else may be the most natural anxiety relief of all.

And although the science is fascinating—long before the research proved it, Dorcas was living it. She didn't need a clinical study—she had a closet full of tunics, a room full of weeping widows, and a reputation for showing up practically and generously. She understood what we so often miss: Generosity isn't just a nice quality, it's a response. A natural outpouring to the extravagant and undeserved generosity Jesus lavishes on us. The kind of generosity that doesn't sit still. It moves. It gives. It acts.

At the end of the day, I don't know if Dorcas's generosity was the reason Jesus (through Peter) spared her life—but it makes me wonder how differently we might view generosity if our life depended on it. And, if science is right, maybe it does.

Don't Miss It

- Generous people give far more than their money.
- Generous people step in when others step back.
- Generous people know their words hold more power than their finances.
- Generous people don't crack open the egg salad at 30,000 feet.

Chapter 9

A Faith Fixer Upper

Well, look at you—halfway through the book! That's farther than I've made it through the Couch to 5K program, intermittent fasting, or any book club that wasn't serving charcuterie boards and talking about everything except the book. (No, Karen, I didn't finish *The Secret Life of Bees*.)

By now, I'm praying you're at least halfway convinced that the seemingly small things matter. Sure, the big things are easy to spot—weddings, funerals, job offers, how you respond when your daughter wants a gap year because college was *just, like, so exhausting and everything*. But what about the little things that barely seem to matter? They're stealth. Sneaky. Easy to miss, and even easier to dismiss. They show up when you're rushing to the band concert, putting out a fire at work, and when you're not even slightly expecting a particular "moment" to count. Yet, they're the scaffolding of a meaningful life.

Speaking of structure, let's talk home makeovers. Give me a sad 1970s ranch, Joanna Gaines in her darling overalls, and a bowl of chips and queso, and I'm suddenly in a committed relationship with my couch for the weekend. I'm a *Fixer Upper* connoisseur (which I just had to ask Siri how to spell, so maybe dial that back a touch). I've watched enough HGTV to dream about demoing every non-loadbearing wall in my home as well as demoing a few people who've suggested the Silos in Waco are overrated. Heresy.

One day, hear me speak this truth people, I'm going to work with Joanna Gaines in some form or fashion. I say this not in a weird "I made a vision board with our faces on it" way (but also yes), but in a "we both went to Baylor University, love Jesus, and feel strongly about magnolia wreaths" kind of way. She'll design open shelving, I'll tell jokes, and together we'll finally dethrone *The Cat in the Hat* podcast. Let's make it happen.

If Joanna's rise to shiplap royalty has taught us anything, it's this: the best spaces—and best stories—start with demolition (bring in Chip). It's the same kind of overhaul that happens in our lives when God starts breaking down all the places we've built without Him. Not to leave us in ruins, but to rebuild something far better. Something with the kind of significance that lasts longer than putting barn doors on every bathroom and hanging those "in this house we ..." signs that make it sound like we're running a cult out of our guest bathroom.

The best spaces—and best stories—start with demolition.

Recently I heard a story in a sermon that I knew belonged in this book. It's not just a story about construction—but building a life with intentionality. Originally I decided it would be the incredible last chapter that ties everything up in a pretty little bow. A sock-it-to-you kind of story that's profound or poignant—or one of those "p" words I mix up.

But the more I thought about it, I realized this story belongs right here in the middle of the book—because that's where so many of us are living. In the middle of parenting. In the middle of marriage. In the middle of caring for our older parents. In the middle of life—looking back, looking ahead, looking around and wondering what really matters (and what doesn't).

So let's think of this chapter as a little intermission. A chance to settle in with a snack and consider a few thoughts. It's also a good excuse to go ahead and put down the book-club book we both know you're not going to finish (unless your book club picked this book—then clearly a very discerning group of women). And let's talk about building a life that really matters, one where even the smallest moments count, and where we don't accidentally miss the stuff that actually lasts.

Built to Last-ish

There was a man who built custom homes. He loved his job. He was unmatched at his craft. He worked for an employer who was very good to him. And as much as he loved building homes for families, he knew that at the forty-year mark, he was going to retire. Hang it up. Move on to greener pastures.

At thirty-five years, he let his company know he only had five more years in him. He sent out emails, announced it in company meetings, and made sure there was absolutely no confusion about his exit strategy. Year thirty-six rolled around, and he marched around the office chanting, "Four more years!" At thirty-eight years, he sent out a memo and ordered a cookie cake announcing, "Only two more years." And then, right on time, year thirty-nine showed up, and the countdown was *really* on.

That last year of his forty-year career felt like it took twenty years, but nonetheless, he finished like a champ. He walked down to his boss's office for the very last time with his head held high, full of the satisfaction only forty years of quality hard work could bring. But somewhere between turning in his key card and grabbing his "World's Best Dad" coffee mug, his boss sheepishly explained that he had just one more request before the builder left. It wasn't a small ask by any means, but the boss needed him to build just one more house. It was for a critically important person, and no other builder had the craftsmanship and expertise to do a job this important.

The almost-retired builder couldn't believe it. He had been announcing his retirement plans for five years, and now it was here, and they had the audacity to spring this on him? Were the cookie cake celebrations, megaphones, and retirement parades not enough to make the point that he was finished? What more could he have done?

Frustrated and fed up, he said no.

But, after much persuasion, in the most reluctant and resentful manner, he conceded. He agreed to build just one more house.

Determined to get the job done quickly, he used whatever laborers were available, even if they weren't the ones he had trusted for years.

He used supplies and finishes that were good enough but not the quality he had insisted on in the past. It took time to do a top-notch job, and time was something he was not willing to sacrifice at this point. He had more pressing plans.

When he finally finished, he stood in front of the house with his boss on what would now *really, really* be his last day. Looking at the house, he knew that on the outside, it looked good—like all the others he had built throughout his illustrious career. But on the inside? Well, it wasn't his best work. He had cut corners and made compromises because his heart wasn't in it. Who could blame him?

His boss thanked him profusely and said he never would have asked him to build this one last home except that it was for such a critically important person—someone who was invaluable to their company. Then his boss handed him the keys and said, "This house is for you. You've been pivotal to this company. *Thank you for all your years of integrity and hard work.*"[1]

The Builder's Dilemma

Here's the truth: We're all building the house we live in. Not with bricks and mortar per se, but with every decision we make. Every time we choose forgiveness over grudge-holding, interruptibility over our timelines, or trust God's plan even when it's hard to see, we're hammering something significant into place. The way we love, the way we define success, the people we surround ourselves with—all of it becomes the framework.

But let's not kid ourselves. Our house is also built just as much by the corners we cut—those moments of grumpiness with our neighbor, selfishness with our money, or distraction with our kids that are easily justifiable in the moment but quietly leave cracks in the foundation of our homes.

The good news is that God is in the business of renovations. He takes our crooked beams and wobbly walls and strengthens them with truth. He patches up the broken places and fills the cracks with His mercy. But it's up to us to stay in the process—to keep showing up with obedience and humility, even when we'd rather call it done and accept the subpar workmanship as good enough. Because a stylish area rug can cover a buckled floor and a little spackle temporarily patches the cracks—but no amount of charm and quick fixes can cover a crumbling foundation (that's almost C. S. Lewis–level quotability right there).

With some reflection, I've realized I've built two houses in my lifetime. The first was built in my first forty years, and it had some truly wonderful features. I have a husband who is godly and faithful, and precious children who are kind, determined, and sometimes boneheads, and incredibly loyal friends—the kind who will show up with a shovel, no questions asked. But as I look closer, I can also see some places where the craftsmanship in my first house was flawed. I started building from the wrong blueprints—ones drawn by saying yes in order to earn people's approval and applause instead of God's, stamped by culture's (and Instagram's) definition of success, and shaded by my ongoing effort to curate a narrative that minimizes my missteps.

It reminds me of a literal house Mike and I lived in during that same season. It was a stately red-brick colonial with big white columns and a massive porch—a home that looked like Atlanta had been picked up and plopped into North Dallas. The outside was stunning. But on the inside, the kitchen was cramped and the living spaces were long and awkward, making it near impossible to host well. The outside screamed *Southern Living* and the inside screamed *gimme a sledgehammer.*

A stylish area rug can cover a buckled floor and a little spackle temporarily patches the cracks—but no amount of charm and quick fixes can cover a crumbling foundation.

Then in my midforties, there came a day of "wreck"oning. One day, I woke up and realized it was time to start caring less about what others thought of me and more about what God thought. That was when Jesus—who'd been waiting patiently for me to come around—stepped in. He graciously began pointing out the spiritual corners I'd been cutting, the superficial finishes I'd chosen for my family, and the cracks in my professional foundation. He challenged me to align who I said I was and who I thought I was with who I *actually* was.

That brings me to one of the few perks of hitting fifty (and it's not the night sweats or the fact that I'm seriously considering a pair of orthopedic walking shoes). The real beauty of the second mile of life is the perspective it offers. I finally have enough life behind me to pause, reflect, and take a long, honest look at the house I've been building all these years. I've slowed down enough to ask a difficult but important question: *Is this the house I actually want to live in?*

That's the question that got me started on building a second house. This one wasn't about appearances or keeping up with anyone else's expectations, but about forgiveness, surrendering my own plans, and choosing obedience, even when it was hard. It included incremental changes like investing in new friendships, finding ministry opportunities, changing careers, and in countless ways reprioritizing our days. The construction was far better on this second house because I followed the plans of a much better builder.

Fittingly, our literal house changed too. We sold the colonial with the awkward floor plan and moved into a home with an open layout, a large kitchen island, and plenty of room for everyone to have a seat at the table (in every respect).

But here's the bottom line about the two houses I've built, both the real and metaphorical: From the outside they both looked pretty good. But on the inside, only one of them was worth living in.

So it's time to wrap up this little intermission—or what my sports-obsessed family would call the seventh-inning stretch. If I could, I would sing "Take Me Out to the Ball Game" and shoot T-shirts into the stands to make sure we *really, really* don't miss this:

Have you considered what kind of house you're building?

Is it pieced together with a makeshift foundation of people pleasing and performance? Are there hidden cracks formed by unforgiveness or shortcuts we've justified far too many times? Have we spent years worrying about the curb appeal while quietly ignoring the cracks behind the walls? Because today is a great day to lay out the blueprints—yours and mine—and hold them up to the light of God's Word. To ask ourselves what truly matters and honestly consider: *Is this the house I really want to live in?*

Or even better, lay the blueprints before God and ask Him: *Is this the house You intended for me to live in?* Because He's not afraid of a faith fixer upper; in fact, He specializes in them.

Don't Miss It

- Curb appeal fades. Foundations last.
- Spiritual "wreck"oning often includes breaking down the old to make room for the new.
- Today's a great day to stop building for applause and start building for eternity. (A lesson from a girl who's tried both.)

Chapter 10

Rocketown, Tom Brady, and Spiritual Calluses

Warning: The following content contains old-school church references, including Christian rock, cutthroat Bible games, and questionable puppet theology. Reader discretion is advised for anyone recovering from trust falls and/or songs inviting us to the Father's big house (with lots and lots of room).

I love church.

Seriously, I L-O-V-E church. And honestly, it's a good thing because I've spent most of my life in the church. Some of you might say, "Yeah, I grew up going to church too," and that's fine and all. But there's a big difference between growing up *going to church* versus growing up *in the church*. Tom and Dorothy (my parents), apparently saw one too many James Dobson videos warning of the atrocities lurking in dark alleys behind the bowling alleys and movie theaters. So for better (most times) or worse (on occasion), they had me and my brothers at church. All. The. Time.

 Church Vans, Bible Drills, and Puppets: What Today's Christian Counseling Is Made Of

I grew up in the middle of 1980s church culture—when the church vans were held together by duct tape and divine intervention, and my hair was shellacked as high as my hopes for a little "fellowship" time with the new kid who visited the youth group last week. Michael W. Smith was raising us up with invaluable life lessons like "a lifetime's not too long to live as friends" and we "could find a life outside of Rocketown." (To this day I have no idea what the Rocketown reference means, yet it still brings a tear to the eye.)

And since I'm totally on a stroll down memory lane, I've decided to provide a bonus litmus test for those of you now questioning if you grew up "in the church."

You know you grew up *in* church if your first kiss was in the third row of a baby-blue church van where the floorboards were so hot you got third-degree burns taking your shoes off on the way home from the spring break ski trip. Bless it—those church vans were death traps filled with a lifetime of memories. Like that time I sparked a heated debate somewhere around Albuquerque, New Mexico, with an unsuspecting youth leader, defending U2 as a Christian band and making my case they were appropriate for the sacred church van speakers. (Please understand I was desperate—there's only so much Petra and Stryper one could take, even if singing "to hell with the devil" felt like a battle cry sprinkled with righteous cussing).

You know you grew up *in* church if, at least once a month, your Sunday afternoon was sacrificed to Bible drills—packed into a room full of cold pizza, New Coke, and awkward preteens who had nowhere better to be. Bonus points if you called them "sword drills," because nothing fights spiritual warfare like me scrambling to find Amos faster than Janna Bowman when the leader barks, "Attention! Present swords! Charge!" Thankfully, the high stress of those Bible drills wasn't wasted because I found Hosea faster than anyone at church just last weekend. Not to mention that I'm pretty sure tabbed Bibles were invented by a bunch of sixth graders scorned from Bible drills.

You know you grew up *in* church if the mention of lock-ins immediately brings back memories of questionable chaperoning at the local YMCA—complete with that inevitable "troubled" teen who somehow snuck in a Ouija board. There's definitely an extra jewel in the crown for the poor youth leader doing the Lord's work giving a 1:00 a.m. devotional to a bunch of kids dead asleep under ping-pong tables ... except for the few of us busy flirting in the sauna room.

You know you grew up *in* church if you don't even slightly flinch at the reference to *puppets* and *ministry* in the same sentence. Saying puppets had a kingdom impact on the scale of Billy Graham revivals might be a slight exaggeration ... but not by much. If there was a fourth great awakening in the modern American church, we owe it in large part to the unsung heroes of the puppet team—countless hours spent crouched on their knees behind makeshift curtains and spray-painted backdrops.

Okay, that should be enough to wrap up my trip down the 1980s church memory lane. But don't you wonder what our kids will say one day about growing up in church culture of the 2000s?

My money is on TikToks mocking the Bible app voices reading Leviticus that we played in the car each day on their way to school. Or QR codes projected on giant screens in pitch-black sanctuaries advertising Tuesday night gatherings with names like "Regenerate" that nobody really understands. Maybe they'll impersonate church bands with their endless bridges, blasting at volumes so loud they set off the noise warnings on their Apple Watches.

I say all this while laughing with church people (not at them) because those memories I shared weren't just funny; they were formative. It was on those youth ski trips that I learned not to settle for anything less than kind, loyal friends who point you to Jesus. It was in Bible studies (and yes, even the Bible drills) where I began to treasure God's Word—the start of a lifelong trajectory of Scripture reading and memorization. And it was in the puppet shows where ... well, bless it—I'm still drawing a blank. But I'm deeply grateful for parents who, in all their Dobson-ness, made sure we *grew up* in the church—didn't just show up at church. It's a foundation I still lean on today (and honestly, they're probably relieved after all that worrying about the shady wisdom of *Three's Company* and *The Love Boat*).

Tom Brady and Spiritual Disciplines: An Unlikely Pairing

If there's one thing my time in church has taught me—besides an appreciation for casseroles topped with cornflakes—it's this: Faith isn't just about church attendance or some surface-level nostalgia from childhood. It's about a deep, daily commitment.

Paul (the apostle, not Rudd) tells us to "work out" our faith in Philippians 2:12. What he's not saying is almost as important as what he is saying. He's not saying we're supposed to work *for* our faith—that's impossible because we're saved by grace. Can't earn it and don't deserve it. But he's suggesting we should work *out* our faith similar to how athletes work out their bodies.

Think about the Olympics for a minute: Let's say you qualified for the 10,000 meter race in the Los Angeles 2028 Olympics. (Sidenote: Once again, I'm so ridiculously unathletic that I don't actually know if the 10,000 meter is a swim, a run, or some terrifying biathlon hybrid. But for the sake of this example, let's call it a run.) Now imagine you have six months to train for the Olympics, and your entire prep strategy is jogging around the block once a week. By anyone's standards, that's not going to cut it. Your effort doesn't match the magnitude of the moment. You've been given the honor of representing your country on the world's biggest stage, and your game plan is limited to a brisk Thursday stroll.

Our faith is no different. We've been given God-sized opportunities—created for us long before we took even one breath. But those moments won't be ours to step into if we treat our spiritual lives like a part-time hobby. If we're called to represent Jesus in a culture desperately in need of eternal truth, a few spiritual laps around the block won't cut it. We've missed it if we think that being spiritually game ready requires anything less than a daily, intentional commitment to walking with Jesus.

Tom Brady is the GOAT of quarterbacks—at least that's what my husband says, and when it comes to sports, he's my authority. Now we are also Dallas Cowboys fans in these parts, which simply means we know a thing or two about disappointment. Yet even in Dallas, we can acknowledge the greatness of Tom Brady. When he was inducted into the Patriots Hall of Fame, he threw out this little gem:

> To be successful at anything, the truth is you don't have to be special. You just have to be what most

> people aren't. Consistent, determined, and willing to work for it. No shortcuts.[1]

Read that again—to be successful you don't have to be special, you just have to be what most people aren't.

It's probably time for another trigger warning because I'm about to drop the phrase *spiritual disciplines*. If you grew up in church, those words make you doze off faster than a sermon on agape versus eros love. So often, we want a deep, abiding relationship with God. We want to sense His direction when our teens are spiraling, or our marriages feel fragile, or we're trying to make a decision that could change everything. And when we see someone who seems to have the kind of peace or spiritual maturity we crave, we sometimes wonder, *What do they have that I don't?*

Applying Tom Brady's words, it's not a matter of talent. It's not luck. It's not being "chosen" in some special way. Instead, it begins with a willingness to do what most people won't. "Consistent, determined, and willing to work for it. No shortcuts."

They're consistently spending time with God—reading His Word, getting alone with Him, praying. Their faith isn't like a January gym membership that fizzles out by February. Paul, in that same letter to the Philippians, says to "press on"—meaning to persevere in our faith, in Scripture, and in walking with Jesus even when it's inconvenient. Because let's be honest: We're tired. We're busy. Life pulls us every which way.

If you'd prefer I make the point through the life of Jesus rather than Tom Brady (and honestly, who wouldn't?), consider this: throughout the Gospels, Jesus often slipped away from the crowds to pray and spend time in solitude. When He faced temptation in the wilderness, He fasted for forty days and met Satan's attacks with Scripture He had memorized.

If Jesus—fully God and fully man—needed to pray, fast, get alone with the Father, and know Scripture inside and out, how much more do we need to make those practices a priority in our own lives?

Netting it out? There are no shortcuts. Deep faith doesn't happen by accident. It happens in private. It happens in prayer. It happens when we show up when we want to give up, when we get quiet when we'd rather scroll, when we open our Bibles instead of our apps, and when we choose the long game over the quick fix.

It's the kind of faith that's built when no one's watching.

Here's the catch: James Clear, author of *Atomic Habits*, says we won't actually change our routines until we're dissatisfied with where we are. He's not wrong. You don't consider a diet until you're spilling out of your skinny jeans and your waistband is whispering, "Please, lay off the queso." You don't start setting your alarm an hour earlier to work on that book until you realize it's due in three months and two paragraphs a day is basically a sad journal entry. (Or maybe that's just me.) The point is: we don't change until staying the same starts to cost us something. And in faith, that cost is often our calling.

Deep faith doesn't happen by accident. It happens in private. It happens in prayer. It happens when we show up when we want to give up.

The good news is the principles of *Atomic Habits* also remind us that spiritual disciplines don't have to be complicated. They're just routines we commit to long enough for them to become habits. It's little things like turning off the radio in the car so you have quiet moments with the Lord each morning. It's putting your Bible by the coffeepot so you're reminded to spend a few minutes in God's Word first thing in the morning. It's a series of tiny, barely noticeable pivots that, over time, yield big spiritual results.

So maybe it's time to consider our faith trajectory for a minute. If we continue praying, reading our Bible, spending time in community, and fasting at the same pace and with the same gusto we're giving it now—will that be a good thing for our relationship with Jesus? Or is it just an occasional lap around the block?

The truth is, we won't have game-time impact if we're skipping the offseason reps (I've never sounded more athletic). In God's kingdom, trajectory trackers are in it for the long game. They're doing the quiet, unseen work—not because they're special (though our identity in Christ certainly is)—but because they're willing to do what most people won't. There are no shortcuts.

The truth is, we won't have game-time impact if we're skipping the offseason reps.

Your Callus Is Showing

I have a friend who travels internationally for ministry. He once told me about something he saw in Egypt: some men have large, unmistakable calluses right on their foreheads. These calluses come from hours spent pressing their heads to the ground in prayer—a physical mark of deep, consistent devotion.

But here's the paradox: Some people want the status of the callus (never thought I'd say that) without putting in the prayer time. They rub their heads on the ground—not to pray but to *look like they do*. They want recognition instead of relationship, and acknowledgment without the inconvenience.

I relate to that more than I care to admit.

I sometimes want peace without the prayer.

Influence without obedience.

Fruit without the faithfulness.

And if I'm really, really honest—the spotlight more than stillness on my knees.

I'm reminded of a time when I had the pinch-me opportunity to speak at an event with one of my faith heroes, Lisa Harper. The night before I flew to Nashville, I was overwhelmed with insecurity. Not just as a speaker but as a mom, a friend, a wife, and frankly, as a follower of Jesus. Imposter syndrome has impeccably bad timing.

I was pacing backstage before my session that night, trying to look composed while mentally unraveling. And then out of nowhere, Lisa came up to me and kindly said, "I want to pray over you." She looked me in the eyes and reminded me that I was loved, seen, and chosen by Jesus—not because of anything I had done or was about to do, but simply because of who He is. And who I am to Him. And then she prayed.

Don't miss this: We can spend a lot of time pacing instead of praying. A lot of time earning a callus that gets us noticed, blind to the callousness that comes with being only marginally devoted.

But faith isn't proven on a platform. It's proven in the quiet moments—when no one's watching, no one's applauding, and no one's handing you a microphone. Its mark is not visible on your forehead—just in your heart.

Don't Miss It

- Jesus practiced prayer, fasting, and solitude—if He needed it, so do you.
- We won't change until staying the same costs us too much.
- Game-time impact requires offseason reps. There are no shortcuts.
- Spiritual shortcuts are like youth group lock-ins: sweaty, slightly traumatic, and usually involve someone sleeping through Bible study.

Chapter 11

Slow and Low: A Barbecue Theology

I never underestimate a woman's ability to get critical information to her man. Whether that's leaving this book open to an exact page with highlights so obvious a Boeing 747 couldn't miss them, or subtly telling her husband on the way to dinner that she feels sorry for her friend's husband "Frank," because he had the audacity to ... (thereafter giving all kinds of instructions and warnings courtesy of fictitious Frank). Either way, may it never be said we don't know how to get our point across.

However, we're also married to men who make high-stakes decisions during the day but can't find the ketchup in the fridge at night—so I'm going to make things easier for everyone by putting together a little list from someone who has been married for a quarter of a century. These are things men who want to stay married should NEVER say:

1. Wow, you must have been hungry.
2. Calm down.
3. What did you do all day?
4. It's really not that hard.
5. Why are you so tired?
6. I'm not a mind reader.
7. Is that *supposed* to be formfitting?
8. They (the kids) never do that when I'm at home.
9. Is that a gray hair?
10. You're acting like my mom.

Let's add to our list any references to that time of the month, hormones, seeming a little "off," and/or language utilizing *big girl panties*. While we're on this topic, can we get rid of the word *panties* altogether? It's heinous. And speaking of words I hate, it's also time to ban the word *lover*. Like let's start a petition, or go to city council, or burn our bras to ensure that we are the change for our grandchildren. Seriously, if you're passionate about climate change, that's amazing and I pray God's speed over you—but as for me and my house, we shall identify and eradicate abominable words. Like *lover*. I speak the necessary and hard truth when I say that not one person cares to hear how you and your *lover* met. Or how you and your *lover* had the best weekend.

I just threw up a little in my mouth.

The other day, I purchased a sign that says, "A recent study found that women who carry a little extra weight live longer than men who mention it." Yes and amen. Then a few days later I ran across a real study suggesting that strong marriages are less about soulmates and more about intentional practices like kindness, compassion, and spending time together.[1] Again, yes and amen.

Soulmates Who Eat Brisket

Twenty-five years of marriage, three kids, two dogs, dozens of jobs, and a few houses later, I wouldn't be honest if I didn't admit there are some moments Mike and I aren't proud of as a married couple. We've both done and said things in the heat of the moment that weren't our best selves. Mike would tell you that one of the most hurtful and disparaging things I've ever said to him was that all barbecue tastes the same to me.

He takes his barbecue very seriously. In fact, the entire state of Texas will pants you in a dark alley for even suggesting that burnt ends are too fatty or that a vinegar-based barbecue sauce trumps our sweet and tangy recipes. We're so serious about barbecue in these parts, that we've broken it into four regions, which include central, east, south and west Texas. Why did we break it up into regions that seem self-evident? That is a question I cannot answer, but stay with me here because a point may or may not be forthcoming.

Simply put, most of what I know about marriage boils down to some barbecue basics. One might call it brisket theology, but that would be weird. So instead let's just say these things are worth considering for those who want to remain ~~lovers~~ in a good marriage.

It's Not Sparkless, It's Just a Stall

The crown jewel of barbecue is *the* brisket—emphasis on *the* because it's not just a cut of meat; it's Texas royalty. You don't earn a coveted spot on *Texas Monthly*'s Top 50 Best BBQ Joints (yes, that exists) by serving decent sausage or ribs, even if they've made grown men weep. No, the real test is brisket. If it's tough, dry, or lacking that almighty smoke ring, Texans will mumble a quick prayer over your smoker, give you a patronizing "bless your heart," and hightail it to the legendary Franklin Barbecue faster than you can say, "But you didn't try my baked beans."

One Sunday, Mike was smoking a brisket, and it was time for our family to head to church. Now, there's a delicate art to suggesting that your pitmaster-scented husband—who's been up half the night tending to a smoker full of meat—might want to shower and change before heading into the Lord's house. God first, brisket second isn't exactly sound theology, but it's a Texas barbecue reality. And I think Jesus gets it.

As we were walking out the door, Mike grabbed his Bible and a trusty little device that looks like a walkie-talkie but is actually a high-tech meat thermometer. It monitors internal temperature, adjusts the fan speed, and even gives an estimated finish time using a probe. (Incidentally, *probe* is also on my list of banned words.) All of this from a tiny box connected to Wi-Fi that doesn't leave Mike's side on smoking weekends.

Honestly, I don't remember much about church that day—except for the moment Mike shot up in the middle of the sermon with the kind of urgency that made every church lady within a ten-pew radius clutch her pearls. I thought maybe he had been moved by the Spirit, but it was actually far less holy. As he bolted out the back of the sanctuary, eyes glued to his walkie-talkie, I heard only one decipherable word: *stall*. And then he was gone, leaving his family stranded at church while he rescued his brisket.

In barbecue terms, a stall is when the temperature plateaus and it looks like the meat has stopped cooking. It's a panicky moment of thinking all the hard work is about to go down the drain. It's basically a brisket breakdown.

In marriage, a stall is when you start asking quiet questions: *Are we still in love? Are we even connecting? Did we lose the spark? Will it ever come back?* It usually shows up when life is at its loudest—when the finances are tight, the calendars are maxed out, and those precious children you once rocked to sleep start making decisions that make you want to lie down in the street.

Can I give you a marriage truth that might not be super popular? Spark is overrated.

Don't get me wrong—it's magical at the beginning. It's the stuff we dreamed about back when we had Jason Bateman posters taped to our bedroom walls and thought love would always feel like butterflies and slow dancing at prom. But spark fades. And when it does, it can leave you wondering if something's broken.

Let me tell you what's better than spark. A man who loves Jesus. The kind who quietly lets go of his dream of a single-digit golf handicap to coach a swarm of four-year-olds who repeatedly score on the wrong goal. The man who is steady and sacrificial, who gives up his dream for a new truck because your daughter finally made the high school dance team she's been praying for and the costumes cost more than rent on your first apartment.

And, yes, he cuts his toenails on his side of the bed, and somehow your left foot always finds the jagged shard at 6 a.m. on the way to the shower. And in that moment, you strongly consider slipping a little antifreeze into his Gatorade. But then you breathe. You laugh. And remember he's gold.

Anyone who's been married longer than a hot minute will tell you: give me the man with the CPAP machine and a quiet faithfulness over the cool guy with a fragile ego and marginal walk with the Lord. And in brisket terms, when the stall hits, the best pitmasters never panic, they just trust the *Texas Crutch*. In its simplest form, that means wrapping the meat in foil to help it push through the stall while keeping it tender, juicy, and headed in the right direction.

The Texas Crutch of marriage? It's choosing to believe that the good far outweighs the hard. It's wrapping our relationship in prayer, humor, grace, and that gritty kind of love that doesn't walk away when things feel slow or stuck. It's watching my husband jump up in the middle of church like a crazy person to go check on his smoker, and then smiling, shaking my head, and thanking the Lord for blessing me with that man (even if I need an Uber to get the kids home from church). And maybe, just maybe, in that moment I feel a tiny flutter in my chest. Something I haven't felt in years. Not the big, cinematic kind of spark. But something quieter. Steadier. Something that makes me realize that what might mistakenly seem sparkless is actually just a stall. And that's just part of the process that leads to something tender and lasting and really, really good.

 The Golden Rule of Barbecue (and Marriage)

Slow and low—this is a nonnegotiable for barbecue success. Translation: don't get all nervous and crank the heat, don't keep messing with it, and by all means, don't rush it. Most of the trouble I've gotten into in marriage has come from reacting too fast and too hot.

Something is left undone, or something he's said (refer back to the aforementioned list of things married men should never say) pushes my buttons. Suddenly, I've gone from 0 to 100 spouting off every ball he's dropped in the last twenty years—like how he remembers every major moment in our marriage based on *who was playing in the Super Bowl that year*. And yes, we got married on Super Bowl weekend 2001 (that's on me)—and no, I'm pretty sure he could not recite to you even one of our marriage vows. But he *can* tell you the Ravens beat the Giants that year, Ray Lewis was MVP, and it was "a strong defensive showing."

Speaking of strong showings, maybe it's time to recognize that our husbands are actually getting it right more often than they're getting it wrong. Honestly, very few of us are married to men who wake up each morning brainstorming ways to ruin our day. They're just humans—flawed but well-meaning—who forget to take out the trash, under-celebrate our birthdays, and sometimes leave up the toilet seat thereby causing us to cuss in the middle of the night. And since God didn't design marriage solely for our satisfaction (but also for our sanctification), we're gifted daily opportunities to exhibit patience and grace. Because let's be honest—it's nearly impossible to do marriage well if we're constantly reacting to every minor offense and spiraling every misstep into a national emergency. Predetermining our attitudes—deciding ahead of time to keep it slow and low—goes a long way. Even when the man you love shamelessly suggests naming your first son Bret Michaels as a tribute to the lead singer of Poison. (For the record, our son's legal name is Michael Brett—which proves I've learned the sacred art of compromise while also navigating my husband's undying affection for '80s hair bands.)

Since God didn't design marriage solely for our satisfaction (but also for our sanctification), we're gifted daily opportunities to show patience and grace.

Slow and low isn't just the golden rule of brisket—it's also a winning strategy for marriage. The ones who don't miss it understand that each day we're handed the choice to either throw gasoline on the fire or keep the heat low and the grace high. We can be angry or kind—but never both. I've lost more ground in my marriage than I care to admit by choosing to be right, at the expense of our relationship. I was microwaving instead of marinating; I reacted fast instead of recognizing that he's human and that, most days, he's doing the best he can. Marriage, like brisket, gets more tender with time. When we step back and let God do His thing, He softens hearts, brings clarity, and speaks truth.

A "Wrong Side of the Tracks" Kinda Love

When Kate was about six weeks old, I experienced what we'll generously call the baby blues—though if I'd gone to the doctor, it likely would've been diagnosed as postpartum depression. The dead giveaway might have been the dozens of mornings I begged Mike to stay home with our jaundiced and fussy newborn so I could go back to my quiet and controllable office in downtown Dallas. A wave also hit me each afternoon around 4:00, when the anxiety would creep in as I dreaded the long nights, the no sleep, and the overwhelming weight of feeling alone with a newborn who was fairly high-strung and not exactly thriving in the nursing department.

Mike, brand-new to fatherhood himself, had no idea how to fix it but knew we needed a diversion. We didn't have a lot of disposable income at the time for a fancy vacation or night nanny to help, so he started planning little outings when he got home from work each day, trying to distract me from what was hard and give me something to look forward to. One day, he suggested we check out a barbecue joint he'd seen on *Texas Monthly*'s Top 50 list. (I believe it would have been classified as barbecue from the west region of Texas for those wondering.) Reluctantly, I agreed, so Mike packed up the car with our newborn in tow, hoping for some tender pork ribs and a few moments of precious peace for his wife.

After what felt like an eternity of a forty-five-minute drive, we finally arrived, and it quickly became clear this wasn't the culinary gem Mike had pictured. It was a rundown shack with a rusted smoker out back and railroad tracks just a stone's throw away. The dimly lit, one-room dining room, with its peeling floors and sticky surfaces, was far from the peaceful haven any first-time, stressed-out mother with a newborn would hope for. But we'd come this far (not to mention we had the place to ourselves), so Mike, ever the barbecue optimist, insisted we give it the ol' college try.

It's funny how those early years of marriage are such a stark contrast to how our world glamorizes relationships today—painting a picture that the best marriages come with soulmates, dream jobs, exotic vacations, well-behaved kids, and picture-perfect homes. If we're not careful, we begin to believe that true love means finding the one who "completes us"—someone who finishes our every sentence and solves problems we've been wrestling with for the last forty years. And while we know deep down that's far from reality, it's easy to look around and feel like everyone else has it all figured out. After all, our neighbor has a new boat, a well-trained dog, and an all-white remodeled kitchen while we're sitting in a proverbial run-down barbecue joint, wiping away tears of discouragement over the gap between the fairy tale we once imagined and the reality we're currently living.

But I can look back with clarity knowing that even when Mike didn't have all the answers, he was present and available and steadfast. And yes, it's true, he might not remember the slightest detail about my wedding dress or the reception flowers I anguished over, but he's shown me time and again what it *really* means to love someone "in sickness and in health," "for richer or poorer," and "for better or worse." He's taught me that perfect marriages aren't built on grand gestures, flawless children, or pristine homes. They're built on small acts of kindness, imperfect barbecue efforts, and showing up—even when you don't know what's wrong, let alone how to fix it.

Each day we're handed the choice to either throw gasoline on the fire or keep the heat low and the grace high.

I wonder how different our marriages would be if we stopped comparing them to the impossible "soulmate" standard—the one that expects a never-ending spark, perfect words at the "right" time, and zero missteps or misunderstandings. What if, instead, we cherished the kind of love that shows up when you're lost in new motherhood, speaks life when your dreams feel stuck on the back burner, and finds ways to bring hope even if it's as simple as some decent food at a run-down shack by the railroad tracks?

A lot has happened in life since that questionable barbecue outing, and I've seen my husband take on a wide array of roles—most of which he's had no training for—to become a baseball coach, foster parent, adoptive dad, math tutor, Bible teacher, fishing partner, prom dress shopper, vacation planner, financial provider, college mover, ministry cheerleader, book writer's editor, field day attender, and tears drier. Time and time again, he's shown up even when the playbook is unclear and the stakes feel impossibly significant. That's a real love. That's a real marriage. That's a real gift. That's what really matters.

(And for what it's worth, I still think all barbecue tastes the same.)

Don't Miss It

- Marriage isn't about constant spark but weathering the stalls and refusing to give up.
- We can choose to be angry or kind—but never both.
- Give me a CPAP and a man who loves Jesus any day over abs and an ego.

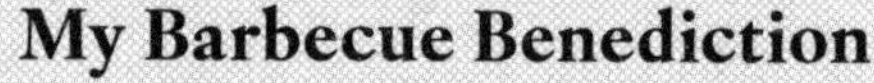

My Barbecue Benediction

Lord, grant me the serenity to accept
the things I can't control—
like brisket that's in a stall and a husband who's
clueless that company is coming in an hour.
Give me the courage to trim the fat but keep the flavor—
whether that's on a slab of meat or
in my salty attitude.
And the wisdom to know
when to dive in or
when to walk away
and let it rest
(especially when
he asks questions
like "What do
you do all day?").
Help me to accept
that stalls and smoke
are part of the
process
and trust that
a slow-and-low
philosophy can make
even the toughest
cuts tender over time.
Amen. And pass the sauce.

Chapter 12

When Life Throws You Two-Star Reviews

Here's the thing about working from my church lobby because I'm too extroverted and undisciplined to sit at home alone all day with laundry, a sink full of dishes, and a horribly behaved dog who barks too much: I meet some interesting people.

Today, I met a gentleman who was walking through the church trying to get in some extra steps. He passed me several times before stopping to ask if by chance I was working on anything related to statistics. Good sir, I can barely *spell* "statistics," much less hold an intelligent conversation about it. Undeterred by my lack of enthusiasm (and knowledge), he excitedly shared that he had spent years working as a statistician before retiring. He had always hoped to find someone in the church lobby who shared his passion for the topic—an event that seems highly improbable. (See what I did there?)

Interestingly, he showed up just as I was starting to write a chapter on gratitude—wondering what on earth I could possibly say about something so essential yet so seemingly obvious. This sweet man launched into a discussion on Bayesian statistics, which in no way seemed relevant to the issues at hand (i.e., him walking and me working). As I was fighting the urge to not get annoyed and panicky because I was up against a deadline, the Lord kindly told me to slow down and listen.

Now, I'm about to drop a high-level statistics lesson that may leave you chanting "Run, Forrest, run!" before I'm done. Undoubtedly, one of you is a statistics buff (which I highly suggest you keep on the DL unless you're in my church lobby), and I'm going to give you permission to cringe during my statistics lesson. But I do believe there's a necessary word on gratitude that came from God via some random retired stats guy. I mean, what are the odds? (These puns are going to need to stop.)

Two of the major approaches to statistics are referred to as frequentist and Bayesian. Frequentists interpret data based on the frequency of events (hence the name). Bayesians base statistics on what they already believe—looking back before looking forward—and adjust it as new evidence comes in. Instead of throwing out what they know, Bayesians refine it—layering new information on top of their existing understanding.

A frequentist might say, "I will be grateful if I see enough repeated evidence of God's goodness to warrant it."

A Bayesian would say, "I believe in God's goodness based on what I already know, and I will process new information through the filter of the faithfulness I've previously experienced."

The frequentists might then say, "Yeah, but what if the new information doesn't weigh in favor of gratitude?"

Let's cut to the chase: Life hands us a mix of wins and losses, joys and heartbreaks. But the more we train ourselves to notice and acknowledge even the smallest reasons for thanks, the more evidence we gather that God is trustworthy. Over time, that stockpile of gratitude shapes our perspective, making it easier to trust Him—even when the next trial comes. In the end, gratitude isn't about ignoring the hard stuff; it's about deciding which evidence gets the final say.

The Bethel Music lyricists are Bayesians at heart, and I'm pretty sure they don't know it (nor do they likely care). But the lyrics of one of my favorite worship songs of all time, "Goodness of God," prove it:

All my life You have been faithful.
All my life You have been so, so good.
With every breath that I am able,
Oh, I will sing of the goodness of God.[1]

If you want a life marked by gratitude, you've got to join the Bayesians' camp. You take what you already know about God's goodness and filter everything new through that lens. Practically, this means looking back at what God has already done in the Bible, in our lives, and all around us. Looking at God's "have beens" reminds us of His faithfulness in the past, helps us recognize His goodness in the present, and gives us confidence in His promises for the future. Our gratitude and trust in Jesus aren't based on perfect conditions or repeated tests; they start with the unshakable truth that He already is.

That's spot-on Bayesian thinking (or that's wrong and I'm completely out over my statistical skis, but either way you get the point).

Those lyrics encourage gratitude not because life has been easy but because time and time again, we've seen God's mercy, His provision, and His presence. We wouldn't need His mercy, provision, and presence if life had been easy. Rather than letting our disappointments or setbacks take the spotlight, we sing of gratitude that's not erased or reset when trials come.

Now just to round it out, I'll also give you a frequentist version of "Goodness of God" that goes like this:

'Cause when life is smooth You've seemed so faithful,
And when things work out You seem so, so good.
With every stress-free breath that I am able,
Oh, I will sing of the goodness of God (unless
that business deal folds next week).

I don't know about you, but I've been known to sing one version on Sunday morning when the music is awesome and I've got all the church "feels" going. And then the very next day—when the school calls, or the market plunges, or the diagnosis comes—my lyrics change.

The more we train ourselves to notice and acknowledge even the smaller reasons for thanks, the more evidence we gather that God is trustworthy.

Defying the Odds

Lots of stories in the Bible make me pause for a variety of reasons. Sometimes because it's hilarious like when Balaam's donkey speaks. Or there's the time when the guy dozed off during one of Paul's sermons and then fell out of the window (we feel you sir; we've all experienced one of *those* sermons). I also stand in solidarity with God when He told Hosea to name one of his kids "Lo-Ammi," which means "not my people." I've got a few Lo-Ammis in my own life—but since it feels rude to name names, I won't.

Then there's the one story that is rarely preached on and often skipped over—but it gets me every time I read it. It's when Jesus healed the ten lepers on His way to Jerusalem (Luke 17:11–19). They weren't just sick men; they were completely cut off from society. Outcasts living on the edge of town in a village, bound together by shared suffering. Men who wouldn't have even associated together as Jews and Samaritans but for their despair. They were forced to yell, "Unclean! Unclean!" as a warning to anyone approaching. They were unwanted, isolated, unworthy in the eyes of their culture, and even believed to be cursed by God.

- Ten men whose clothes were burned rather than washed
- Ten men completely cut off from their culture
- Ten men with no dignity
- Ten men with a death sentence

Then Jesus came. He saw them. He spoke to them. He told them to go show themselves to the priests—and, as they went, they were healed.

But only one came back to thank Him. Just the one.

- One returned to the miracle worker.
- One threw himself at the feet of his Savior.
- One shouted in gratitude the way he had once shouted, "Unclean!"
- One exchanged shame for worship.
- One received not just physical healing—but eternal life.

Jesus said to him, "Your faith has made you well." And with those words his heart was also healed.

It goes without saying (which you've learned by now means I'm going to say it) that without Jesus, we're no different from the ten outcasts. We, too, are unclean. We, too, are on the outside looking in—with no real belonging and a death sentence hanging over us.

It may not be leprosy, but let's be honest here, we should all be walking around yelling, "Alcoholic!" "Gossip!" "People pleaser!" "Judgmental!" "Jealous!" "Materialistic!" "Unforgiving!" We carry sins that isolate us, shame that silences us, and habits that should justifiably have Jesus calling us Lo-Ammi.

Yet He still heals us and claims us as His own.

But so often ... we don't go back.

We're the ones Jesus was talking about when He asked, "Were not all ten cleansed? Where are the other nine?"

We take the miracle—but miss the Messiah.

We receive the gift—but forget the Giver.

We accept healing to our body—but gloss over the condition of our heart.

We miss the chance to be the *one* who falls down in gratitude to the *One*.

 "Meh" Isn't Even a Word

Most authors will tell you that there's typically a book-writing moment when you find yourself staring at a blank screen, the cursor blinking, wondering, *Who thought it was a good idea to give me a two-book deal in the first place?*

Seriously, not one of my grade-school teachers EVER said I was a great writer, much less encouraged me to set my sights on being an author. Never once was one of my law school professors overheard telling the faculty, "Forget about her contracts grade; she's going to write something amazing one day." Heck, my kids don't even ask me to edit their school essays because they believe their dad is the best choice in the house. And I don't even disagree. Statistically speaking, I'm the last person who thought I'd be writing books.

So recently, during a particularly colossal writing slump, I decided I needed a little book-writing pep talk. As one does, I went straight to Amazon and scrolled through the reviews for my first book as a little pick-me-up. *What could possibly go wrong with going to the internet for encouragement, right?*

There were 67 reviews and 130 ratings on Amazon for *Life Is Messy, God Is Good*. And most said nice things like "encouraging," "relatable," "humor and wit is unmatched." But then there was one.

There's always *the one.*

The two-star review I'm ~~cursing~~ referring to is titled, "Honestly kind of meh." I'll spare you the full rant and give you the highlights:

> If you have experienced any sort of hard or trauma in your life, this book is definitely NOT for you. If you have experienced a good upbringing, have good friends, have a good nuclear family and have some things here or there that are annoyances, then this book is for you. I felt like it was written in a privileged setting and has no real connection to those that may not have good parents and struggle to find good friends or a good marriage.

I'm fine, everyone, really, I'm fine.

With a little time to reflect, a statistical analysis of how many people will actually read that review, and a few Xanax (kidding), here's my gratitude takeaway:

If we know Jesus as our Lord and Savior and our eternity is secure, then we *are* privileged. Having our names written in the Book of Life is the ultimate privilege. Everything else can't help but flow from that truth, including gratitude. This is not me coming from a defensive posture because someone didn't like my writing—heck, at best, that review is from one of my grade-school teachers; and at worst, it was written by one of my kids!

But here's a truth that's easy to miss: Nothing drains our gratitude faster than fixating on the one negative when we've got 65 positives staring us in the face. Said differently, when you've got a 65:1 ratio of good to bad, focusing on the one negative is betting on the wrong odds. (That's a statistic even I can understand.)

Life is full of two-star reviews. You may not have been slayed on Amazon, but we all have a criticism, rejection, or heartbreak. We've all carried around the sting of someone's harsh words or the restless nights wondering what the future holds.

Nothing drains our gratitude faster than fixating on the one negative when we've got 65 positives staring us in the face.

Short version?

A heart rooted in gratitude is our greatest defense when the two-star reviews of life threaten to overshadow the five-star faithfulness of the One who walks with us through it all.

Don't Miss It

- Gratitude doesn't ignore the hard stuff but filters which evidence gets the final say.
- "Meh" moments are good reminders that we serve a five-star God in a two-star world.
- Only one leper came back. Be the one.

Chapter 13

Stuck between a Ramp and a Hard Place

Have we established at this point that I was an attorney back in the old days? Since there were no lawyers in my family growing up, I knew the sum total of nothing going into law school. So I created a little script in my head that being a lawyer was going to be like joining the cast of *Ally McBeal* (minus that weird dancing baby that represented her ticking biological clock). I imagined a law practice that primarily focused on the romantic and personal lives of the main characters (i.e., me and my new law friends) with lots of action and, if all went as planned, very little law.

Okay, maybe I'm dating myself with the *Ally McBeal* reference. Let me try again.

I thought being a lawyer would be like *Suits*. I'd be the female version of Mike Ross (with an actual law degree), mentored by a brilliant Harvey Specter–type boss. Each day would end with a dramatic mic-drop moment where I put someone in their place and exited the room dramatically in my fabulously tailored pencil skirt. Oh, and I was going to have a snappy legal assistant like Donna, who knew all the office drama and had perfectly timed quips like, "You don't have my sympathies for being so [darn] stupid." (Donna's salty language is edited here because my parents will read this.)

Well, in an unfortunate turn of events, real-life law firms actually care about ... wait for it ... the law. There was zero appreciation for my snappy one-liners or the beginnings of a great pencil skirt collection. Instead, they handed me a two-hundred-page discovery binder and told me to be in Texarkana by the next morning. And the biggest travesty? My Donna wasn't some quick-witted assistant. Nope. His name was Denny, and his cubicle was decorated with a calendar featuring his cats in seasonal costumes.

Six or so years into my "illustrious" legal career, I'd managed to score some major wins personally but very few professionally. I had a great husband, two awesome kids, and a real knack for pretending to care about billable hours and associates' meetings. Somewhere around that time I also started praying that the Lord would give me a new calling or direction or something that didn't require me to drive downtown every day to an endless loop of billable hours and settlement documents. On a more spiritual note, I had that sense of holy discontent I had heard about growing up in church, and I had suspicions the Lord was actually authoring a new chapter in my life.

One day I was running late for work and having a morning that neither *Ally McBeal* nor *Suits* even slightly warned me about—my kids were a mess, traffic was ridiculous, and I was a far cry from fashionable in my Casual Corner polyester suit that made a hazmat suit look downright sultry. I had been on the phone with a friend as I pulled into the parking garage, probably saying something really important like, "Wait, are you saying people who aren't interested in the law don't typically go to law school?" Normally, I parked on the first or second level, but since I got there late, all the good spots were taken. So I sped up to level seven, flying around corners like I was Jason Bourne. Then, out of nowhere, I heard this ridiculously loud scraping sound above me. My car stopped so fast that my Diet Coke went flying into the back seat (quite the graceful entrance when you're already late to work).

What I now know—but desperately wish I'd known five seconds earlier—is that the higher levels of this particular parking garage have lower ceiling clearances than where I usually park. Translation: My SUV didn't quite clear the roofline. I ended up perfectly, and humiliatingly, wedged between the level-seven ramp and the ceiling—a tighter fit than wearing Spanx on Thanksgiving Day.

And I'll save you some time: There's not a chapter in your car's owner's manual titled, "So You've Lodged Your Vehicle between Two Immovable Structures." Nor, for the record, do law schools prepare one for this. Torts? Yes. Constitutional law? Of course. But "Parking Garage Situational Awareness and the Laws of Physics"? Nowhere in the curriculum.

I tried reverse. Nothing. Forward? Nada. My SUV was as stuck as I was in my seemingly dead-end job. A few minutes later, the garage attendants arrived to assess the situation. Read: Silently judge my life choices. Turns out, this wasn't going to be a quick fix. And just to really "drive" home the humiliation, it was nearly lunchtime, and thanks to me, no one could get in or out of the upper decks. I had single-handedly brought the entire parking garage to a standstill (while also killing Chipotle's bottom line for the day).

There I sat in the driver's seat, watching helplessly as a small crowd of strangers gathered around my car like it was a body at a crime scene. A few picked up the shattered remains of my luggage rack, while others stood in a deep, furrowed-brow huddle, clearly one YouTube tutorial short of an actual plan.

After what felt like an eternity, I hit my limit. With the exasperation that only a woman late to work, wearing half a can of Diet Coke, and trapped in a wedged SUV can summon, I blurted out, "What in the world could possibly be taking so long?"

The Waiting Game

There are few things I hate more than waiting. I'm a doer by nature. The problem is that most of life's best things require a wait: your wedding day, the Slinky Dog ride at Disney World, childbirth, and your bangs growing back after a failed attempt to reinvent your high school self. Trust me, I've tried to rush all four and it didn't end well. Especially the bangs.

It doesn't help that we live in a Grubhub-Amazon-Spotify kind of world where waiting has been escorted from the premises. Can you even imagine our kids waiting like we used to in the old days? Sitting by the radio for hours hoping to hear their new favorite song? Actually driving to Taco Bell and standing in line to get the Cool Ranch Doritos Taco they've been craving? These are children who think buffering is a personal attack. We'd blow their minds if we told them about the olden days when we had to go inside a pharmacy when we ran out of deodorant. And then—deep breaths—stand in line to pay for it. With cash. Madness.

Ironically, as much as I hate waiting, I am currently in the throes of an intense season of waiting. Our daughter is waiting to find out where she will be accepted into law school. (Believe you me, I've warned her repeatedly that *Suits* is a scam, yet somehow she hasn't made an abrupt 360. Or is it 180? I always get that wrong. But I digress.) Our older son is a senior in high school and waiting to hear back on college acceptances. Mike and I are waiting on the Lord to move some significant mountains both professionally and personally. And as I sit here tapping my fingers, praying for the Lord to do what only He can do, I'm on the verge of another parking-garage-sized meltdown wondering, *What in the world could possibly be taking so long?*

Because if Jesus can part the seas and move the mountains (or provide the job, bring the husband, or cure the anxiety in our lives)—why doesn't He just do it? I say this as a girl who truly believes that Jesus can orchestrate any miracle in an instant all while working *all things* for His glory and our good. I've seen Him do it. I can testify to it. Yet as much as I trust His sovereignty, so often I'm left questioning His methodology and timing.

When a Car Problem Is Actually a Perspective Problem

When you think about being stuck in a season of waiting, I'm assuming the book of Habakkuk doesn't just pop into your head? Me neither. So, just in case you've forgotten what it's about—or even where it is in the Bible (my Bible drill days are coming in clutch right now)—here's the quick version: Habakkuk was fed up. He was watching his country, Judah, fall apart with all its corruption and chaos, and he kept saying, "Hey, God! When are You gonna do something about this mess? Seriously, how long do I have to keep calling out before You answer?" (I feel you, Habakkuk. I really do.)

Then God finally responds, but it's not the answer Habakkuk wanted. God says He's going to use Babylon—basically the worst of the worst—to straighten things out. And that just throws Habakkuk for a loop because, come on, using bad guys to fix the bad guys? Two wrongs a right do not make.

But Habakkuk's response to God is interesting. He says:

> I will stand my watch
> And set myself on the rampart,
> And watch to see what He will say to me,
> And what I will answer when I am corrected.
> (Hab. 2:1 NKJV)

Just in case you haven't gotten frustrated recently and started ranting about a rampart, let me explain. Standing on a rampart means Habakkuk is putting himself at a high vantage point, like a watchtower. He's getting in a place where he's best able to wait for God to move. He knew that his view was clouded by frustration, confusion, and a serious case of "God, what is even going on right now?" Sound familiar? So instead of spiraling at ground level, he's positioned himself in the best place he knew to wait and watch with expectation.

Sitting deep in the bowels of that parking garage, my view was also pretty limited—literally and figuratively. All I could see in front of me was a very stuck car and the end of my dignity. People were circling, whispering, picking up shattered bits of my roof rack, but it seemed as though no one was actually doing anything. It was maddening.

What I didn't realize at the time was the building manager had called a structural engineer to come assess whether my little mishap had, in fact, compromised the integrity of the building. Who knew that lodging your vehicle into the top of the parking garage like a missile had the potential to compromise the structural integrity of an entire office building? Eventually, after the inspection was complete and the building was officially deemed *not* about to collapse, they greenlit the next step: a heavyset garage attendant was called to jump up and down on my running board as they deflated my tires so I could escape the humiliation of the garage.

Some situations take a decade or so to decide whether they are hilarious or mortifying. Ten years later, I'm still on the fence with this one. But don't miss this: Sometimes God uses the waiting to examine the structural integrity of our faith. From the parking garage level, we only see the stuckness—the delay, the setback, the why-is-nothing-moving moment. But from above, God is busy rounding out our rough edges, redirecting the deepest desires of our hearts, and bridging the gaps between our Sunday theology and Tuesday afternoon reality.

In the wait, He's very often weaving together a story for the benefit of many, even when the cost is a delay for one. Because God knows, in His infinite wisdom, that moving the mountain before checking the foundation can cause the whole thing to come crashing down. So what feels like a frustrating delay is not punishment—but preparation—for what He's building next.

Hebrews 11:6 says, "Without faith it is impossible to please God." Faith means trusting that God knows best, both in His plan and timing. A deep faith isn't forged overnight—it usually involves waiting. It comes as we learn to trust Him even if it costs us time we don't care to give, delays we don't want to experience, and a new perspective we didn't ask to see.

What feels like a frustrating delay is not punishment—but preparation—for what He's building next.

Our buddy Habakkuk didn't like the answer God gave and was tired of the waiting game, but he took to higher ground. Sitting in the hurt and frustration of unanswered prayer has a way of distorting our view—ground level tends to do that. Maybe it's time we follow suit. Instead of fixating on the stuck car, the unpaid bill, the dead-end job, or struggling child, what if we climbed to higher ground? What if we left the ramp for the rampart, seeking a broader vantage point to wait doggedly for God to answer in ways only He can, on a timeline only He knows?

Taking to higher ground isn't just metaphorical; it's practical. Sometimes it means carving out a quiet spot to pray and recalibrate. Other times, it means closing apps, quieting the noise, and walking away from the comparison trap. More often than not, it means choosing to bring your frustrations to God instead of unloading them in the group chat. And most days? It means anchoring yourself in Scripture, trading the question "Why, Lord?" for "What are You asking me to learn here?"

There was one other kick in the pants for Habakkuk: Along with a new perspective, he was also given a new pace. He prayerfully asked God for a resolution to his problems, and God assured him that He was going to answer his prayer. But God also gave a huge caveat that it would not happen until "the appointed time." The Hebrew word for appointed is *moed*, and it means the unstoppable time of God.

That morning I was flying through the parking garage because I was late for the "real work" happening on the twenty-fifth floor of a law firm. Yet, as it turns out, the *real* work wasn't in a high-rise office but in a parking garage basement. That's where God, who was far more interested in refining my soul than advancing my career, patiently re-stirred the affections of my heart, slowed me down, humbled me, and prepared me for how He was going to answer my prayer with a new direction.

Months later, I walked away from my law "career"—a step of obedience that set us on a path to foster care, led us to JB, and reshaped how we live day to day. But from parking garage level, none of it made sense at the time. It took higher ground, with a clearer view, to see how what once felt like a frustrating delay was actually God's perfect preparation. His *moed* was better.

Speaking of JB, Mike has a thing he does with him most days. It's a simple exchange but also a reminder of what we've walked through to get here. It goes like this:

> "What's your name?"
> "JB Yanof."
>
> "What do we do?"
> "Hard things."

"What do we not do?"

"Give up."

Waiting and trusting—those are two of the hardest things we'll ever do in faith. They don't come with tidy timelines or clear explanations. But the ones who don't miss it understand they are the training ground where God shapes our courage, hones our character, and prepares us for things far better than we anticipated.

What once felt like painful silence turned out to be God's most intentional movement. So in big moments and small ones, we—like JB—remember who and whose we are. We remember that with God, we can do hard things (like wait). And no matter what comes our way, we never give up because we know the One who holds our future is already there, working all things for good.

Waiting and trusting are the training grounds where God shapes our courage, hones our character, and prepares us for things far better than we anticipated.

Not the First or the Last

A few days after the parking garage incident, I ran into a policeman as I was walking to my car. He stopped to ask if I was the one who knocked the top off my car. Sheepishly, I admitted that I was in fact the one. I was expecting a lecture, but instead, he said, "Oh yeah, you're not the first one." At least one person a month had gotten stuck since he started working there. Turns out, the building manager was in the process of installing big warning signs and flashing lights to warn future drivers. Not to brag, but how many people can say their reckless driving led to public safety upgrades? You're welcome, Dallas.

Whatever we're waiting on. Wherever we're discouraged. In whatever way God is molding and shaping us while we wait, we're not the first—and won't be the last. Let Habakkuk be our flashing light and bold signage, reminding us to slow down, get to higher ground, and trust in the unstoppable timing of God.

God's *moed* is so much better than ours—don't miss it.

Don't Miss It

- Sometimes God uses the waiting to examine the structural integrity of our faith.
- God's delay for one is often for the benefit of many.
- When nothing seems to be moving, don't assume God isn't.
- Good news: God's *moed* won't come a second too soon. Bad news: It might include a hefty fella jumping on your SUV.

Chapter 14

Home Is Where the Sopapillas Are

My brother had lost his job. He spent just shy of three decades with the same company. With one phone call and a thirty-minute meeting, it all ended. Long before he knew this shocking turn of events was on the horizon, he had made plans to go back to our hometown for a few days. He rented a small house in El Paso, Texas, which is approximately ten hours from where most of our family lives now. Although the timing of the trip seemed inopportune in the wake of such a career setback, the food, the mountain views, the open space to ride his motorcycle, and especially the memories drew him back home.

He called each of us to share the disappointing news about his job and his plans to be away for a few days, assuring us not to worry. Our thoughtful parents, sensing he might need some company, offered to join him, and he gratefully accepted. My other brother, his twin, decided to make the trip from Colorado. With four-fifths of our family embarking on this journey together, I knew *I didn't have time not to go.*

Moments with just the five of us—my nuclear family—are rare and fleeting. And with our precious eighty-six-year-old dad bravely fighting Alzheimer's, these moments feel even more significant. And numbered.

The moment my flight touched down in El Paso—the border town that shaped so much of who I am—the memories rushed in. Big ones, like being so nervous that I projectile vomited after my first real kiss, and small ones, like the time when a few guys from high school wrote a song for my mom (who had just had a breast biopsy) and walked right into her bedroom to sing this little ditty:

Dottie Dottie, all laid up,
we came by to cheer you up.
Not real sure just what is wrong,
but just sit back and hear our song.

When I met up with my family, we all agreed there were a few places we had to visit while we were in town.

Almost immediately, we set out to drive by the one-story white stucco home where we spent most of our childhood. Although the exterior is a little weathered now, those walls hold a lifetime of stories. Like the time our mom caught the bathroom on fire with a candle during a dinner party, or when my brothers started a garage band called

Paris (because they were so international and everything) that made the neighborhood dogs form a support group, or the night my dad chased down a skunk in his boxers (my dad, not the skunk) and then trapped it under a trash can. Oh, and let's not forget the time my mom completely lost it in the kitchen and dropped a bad word because my brothers were being heinous teenagers and she'd hit her holy limit. It wasn't a *really bad* word, but still, it was something we'd never heard come out of Dorothy's mouth before or since. And no, we will never let her live it down.

Next, we went by the church where I learned a whole lot about Jesus, mainly from our pastor, Dr. Levi Price. I also learned a whole lot about kissing boys from the same pastor's son, which is a good reminder that spiritual truth coupled with practical life lessons can walk hand in hand. Our youth group choir did a dinner musical one time called "Friends Forever," and surprising to everyone, I got the lead solo. I belted out Michael W. Smith's song "Friends" so earnestly that it brought tears. Tears are tears, folks, and I chose to believe people were moved, not startled. Unfortunately, one time in a "go big or go home" moment, I also sang "Via Dolorosa" in front of the entire church. (I should have gone home. I owe Sandi Patty a personal apology.)

At some point along the journey, we got hungry and made a stop at our favorite childhood restaurant, Leo's, for the famous number four combination plate with two cheese enchiladas and a taco. The memories—coming home from college and heading straight to Leo's for dinner, gathering with family friends for Sunday lunch, or being treated to a meal by our beloved adopted grandfather, Ed—are what makes this restaurant more than just a place to eat; at some point it just became part of our story. On a more serious note, they give you free sopapillas after your meal, and all you need to know is that pouring honey over fried dough covered with cinnamon and sugar is a religious experience. And not the kind that leaves a bad taste in your mouth like when a fifteen-year-old girl in a border town boldly attempts the Spanish portions of "Via Dolorosa."

Then we passed by the neighborhood where I took piano lessons. My piano teacher was incredibly hardcore and … I was not. I lost count of the number of times she sent me to wait outside on the curb for my mom because I hadn't practiced and was wasting her time. It's too bad because my mom is an amazing pianist (pronounced pee-un-ist and therefore added to my banned-word list) and she had great aspirations for me to follow in her footsteps. I, on the other hand, was a talented jokester with no interest in learning theory and dressing up for recitals at the Women's Club where Courtney Brown brought down the house with her piano prowess, and I just brought down people's expectations with my lack of progress.

Perhaps it goes without saying that my piano career was short-lived. I took lessons for eight excruciatingly long years, and all I have to show for it today is a few measures of "Arms of Love" by Amy Grant (tell me you grew up in the '80s without telling me you grew up in the '80s) and a recurring nightmare that I can't end "Moonlight Sonata" in front of seventy-five glaring parents.

It feels like now is as good of time as any to air a few long-standing grievances with my esteemed piano teacher.

A Letter to My (Now Deceased) Piano Teacher

Dear Mrs. W.,

I really did want to learn to play the piano, I promise.

I mean, my mom was the church pianist, for crying out loud. I have musical brilliance running through my veins. All systems appeared to be a go for me becoming a mini-Mozart. Except that you were a buzzkill. And kinda mean, if we're honest.

Nobody wants to study music theory for one hour each week while our friends are meeting boys at the mall.

Nobody wants a passive-aggressive metronome turned on when we're simply trying to jazz up a classical tune.

Nobody wants to go to the "Women's Club" for a recital on Saturday afternoons wearing pantyhose—although that sherbet/ginger-ale punch concoction you made was top-tier.

Now I will admit I wasn't the model student, and a few apologies are in order.

I'm sorry I suggested we "play it by ear" when you were freaking out about my concert piece.

I'm sorry I failed every single theory test you made me take for eight consecutive years, leading you to suggest to my mother that I might have learning differences.

I'm sorry my mom found you at Luby's Cafeteria ten years later, after I graduated from law school, and reported back that I did not have learning differences but was simply unchallenged.

And if it makes things any better, I still remember that "every good boy deserves fudge" is the acronym for the treble clef notes and "good boys do fine always" for the bass clef. Honestly, based on your acronyms, I'm starting to believe you thought I was a boy. And even though I'm a firm believer that haircuts don't lie, please know that my short sides and frizzy top were totally on trend for the '80s.

Last thing: It's never not funny to say excuse me when the piano bench creaks. I stand by that.

Signed,
Anonymous

We also visited a small cemetery where most of our parents' extended family are buried. If you've been wondering at what age you start including cemeteries in your hometown visits, apparently, it's my age. We walked up and down the rows and read the names of people on headstones, including those of my grandparents. We overheard our mom and dad talking about how *these* people (pointing to a headstone) had the strongest marriage, and *these* people were great hosts of an annual fish fry, and *these* people were pillars of faith in the community. Even my dad, who now struggles to remember so much, shared stories about the lives in that cemetery who had shaped his own.

Going back to El Paso made me miss the simpler days. Back when the stories we told centered around my brothers' teenage antics, not lost jobs. When my dad used to buy motorcycles and snowmobiles to create memories—not spend his days struggling to recall them. When my piano failures came from a lack of interest, not from the significant learning differences facing our youngest son. I even wished for one more day without email—especially after one came in during our trip with hard news I chose not to open.

The Broken Road

Driving by my old church, I remembered a really, really old couple who taught my sixth grade Sunday school class. I don't remember their names anymore, but I do remember how every single week they made us work on memorizing the same passage of Scripture. If they had asked my piano teacher, they would have known that I had a well-documented deficit for learning seemingly boring information. But they were no dummies; they bribed us with candy and donuts each time we learned another verse.

Apparently, their tactics worked because, as annoyed as my twelve-year-old self was with their Scripture memorization fixation, my fifty-three-year-old self is about to recite those same verses completely from memory:

> Let not your heart be troubled; you believe in God, believe also in Me. In My Father's house are many mansions; if it were not so, I would have told you. I

> go to prepare a place for you. And if I go and prepare a place for you, I will come again and receive you to Myself; that where I am, there you may be also. (John 14:1–3 NKJV)

I wish I could ask them why, of all the verses in the Bible, they were so bound and determined for a bunch of preteens to memorize John 14. (But since they were like two hundred years old when I was in sixth grade, we can safely assume that's a question for heaven.)

Yet as I look more closely at the passage and the verses leading up to John 14, I notice Jesus had just spent the evening washing His disciples' feet. Over dinner He was trying to help them understand that He'd be leaving them. But they couldn't seem to grasp how His heavenly calling required an earthly death. Jesus gave them the kindest instruction: He said, "Let not your heart be troubled." He was giving assurance that this world—this broken, unexpected, oftentimes unfair, and temporary place—was not their final home.

All these years later, I think I finally understand why that *elderly* couple was so insistent we learn those particular verses. I'm guessing they had lived enough life to know that one day, that fresh-faced, naive, and horrible pianist of a twelve-year-old girl would reach a point where the place she called home would feel heavy and crushing. That she would visit cemeteries—the symbolic ones where she buried the dream for her family's perfect health, upward job trajectories, and kids with no childhood struggles; and the very literal ones, where she would bury dear friends and family, with reminders that memories may fade but legacies do not. The journey she was on would feel discouraging, and, like the disciples, she would struggle to understand how a heavenly calling could sometimes feel like an earthly death. My Sunday school teachers probably knew there would be moments when I'd feel overwhelmed and ready to give up. But they didn't want us to miss it—knowing that the Lord is preparing a new, incredible home for us and He will return to take us there one day.

If anyone can empathize with a tumultuous road to heaven, it's the man who walked the road to Calvary.

Recently there was an ad campaign on TV that simply said, "He gets us." It found it to be reassuring—the reminder that Jesus gets us when the road back home is filled with laughter, and great food, and a house that holds some of our fondest memories. Yet He also gets us when the road is broken and the career door shuts, the memory fades, and the discouraging news is waiting in an email we don't even have the nerve to open. If anyone can empathize with a tumultuous road to heaven, it's the man who walked the road to Calvary. He left this earth ostracized, beaten, and crucified with a crown of thorns—but in the words of "Via Dolorosa":

He chose to walk that road out of
His love for you and me
Down the Via Dolorosa, all the way to Calvary.[1]

(Notice I was smart enough to write it this time and not sing it. That being said, I can and will pull out my Spanish version upon request.)

When the Silence Is Deafening

In a recent sermon, my pastor talked about Beethoven. Naturally, I perked right up since I too have a distinguished piano background. He reminded us that by age forty-five, Beethoven was completely deaf. For a man whose entire life revolved around music, it was a devastating loss. At first, he was outraged and would bang on his piano with increasing fury trying to somehow hear the notes. And then eventually he became depressed, even contemplating ending his life.

But then, after some time, he went back to writing.

He didn't give up because it was unfair.

He didn't give up because it was too hard.

In fact, some of his most iconic and transcendent compositions were written *after* he lost his ability to hear. Because even when he couldn't hear the chords, he still knew their sound.

Arthur C. Brooks observed, "Deafness freed Beethoven as a composer because he no longer had society's soundtrack in his ears."[2] That will preach as we're living in a world overflowing with Netflix binges and Instagram reels.

But that's the thing about our hardest losses—they strip away the noise and leave behind what matters most.

I think of my dad and his declining memory. Although his short-term memory is suffering and daily tasks are more complicated than they used to be—walking in the cemetery that day, row by row, he had no problem remembering people, their stories, and their faith.

I think about my brother losing his job and the hurt and unknown he's facing in the days ahead of him. Yet as our family rallied around him for a few days back home, he was reminded that he never walks the road alone.

I think about myself and raising kids with setbacks and struggles. How something as simple as passing by my old church was a reminder that the Lord has been engraining His hope and truth in my life for as long as I've known.

I wonder what we're writing in the silence.

That's the thing about our hardest losses—they strip away the noise and leave behind what matters most.

On the other side of loss and discouragement, will it be said that we've given up? That we've declared life is unfair? Will we be at the Women's Club banging on our proverbial piano in frustration for what should have never been?

Or will our best work be on the other side of navigating the hardest of circumstances? Will we still know the chords of His grace even when life has clouded our ability to hear them as clearly?

What was true in sixth grade holds even truer in my life today: Jesus is preparing a new home for us—one with no more pain, no more loss, no more tears, and no more struggles.

This truth allows us to write even more beautiful music in the midst of our deepest loss. The ones who don't miss it understand that even if the road back to our ultimate home is filled with pink slips, painful diagnoses, broken relationships, failed dreams, and unopened emails—Jesus is still whispering, "Do not be troubled. I go to prepare a place for you with no more tears, no more pain, and full of sopapillas." (Loosely translated, of course.)

Don't Miss It

- The setbacks of this life remind us that our home was never here in the first place.
- Memories fade, legacies do not.
- Sometimes God uses loss to lead us home—and sometimes He uses sopapillas. Trust the journey.

Chapter 15

Spicy TED Talks and a Masked Yes

In my lawyer days I took tons and tons of depositions. Basically, a deposition is when the attorneys in a lawsuit get to ask a witness, under oath, about the facts of the case. A court reporter is in the room to take it all down so there is a permanent record of the testimony. Oh, and sometimes they even have fancy cookies in the room, which is mainly why I attended depositions (well, and the fear of being fired if I didn't show up). You also need to know that I speak so fast that a court reporter once told me her stenotype machine was going to catch on fire if I didn't slow down. My apologies.

Depositions allow attorneys to understand what a witness will say at trial, while preventing anyone from changing their story later. You get one shot to tell your story; after that, the testimony is fair game for the lawyers to use however they need it moving forward in the case.

For years, I flew all over the country taking depositions for a large company that my law firm represented. The type of work was called products liability, and in essence, my job was to help defend a product that the other side claimed was defective. One of the products my law firm was defending at the time was a mask. I can't say much more about it because of attorney-client privilege, but even more so because you would fall asleep. Suffice it to say, individuals who wore these masks on jobsites alleged that they contracted respiratory illnesses because the masks didn't work.

During the depositions, I would ask the plaintiff a million questions about the masks. I could do it in my sleep. What did they look like? Did you take your mask off? Did your jobsites ever run out of them? Do you know the brand of the mask? Did you wear other brands? What work were you doing when you wore them? You get the point.

The depositions all run together except for this one time when I encountered an older guy who was very feisty and obviously didn't enjoy the legal process (who can blame him) and surely didn't appreciate lawyers (again, who can blame him). He had been answering questions for hours by the time it was my turn, and he was over it. So I finished up my cookie and began my litany of questions about the mask like I'd done a million times before. But it didn't take me long to realize this guy had an agenda; he was going to make sure I knew that he thought our product was terrible and that's why he was sick. It was going to be a long day.

But then something funny happened that had never happened in the hundreds of previous depositions I'd taken: Midway through his testimony, he mentioned he was a smoker. I started asking how much he smoked and how this smoking habit worked on jobsites. I gleaned they weren't allowed to take smoke breaks, so I was curious how he beat the system. With the confidence of someone who believed he was the model for OSHA workplace safety, he let me know that he *always* wore the required protective mask. However, he also smoked most of the day, so he had to cut a hole in the middle of the mask so his cigarette could hang out.

Someone please pass the cookies.

The attorneys in the room tried not to make eye contact with each other for fear of laughing. His lawyer jumped in and agreed to let my client out of the case immediately because, well, there was a gaping hole in his case (pun intended).

I couldn't help but feel sorry for the poor guy who couldn't grasp why cutting a hole in his mask—*the very mask he was claiming failed to protect him from respiratory illness*—was an issue. As I was leaving the room, I overheard him saying to his lawyer, "*Yes*, I wore that mask every day, *but* I also needed a smoke."

That my friends, is the danger of the "yes ... but" mentality. Sometimes you inadvertently become the butt of the joke.

Our Masked Yeses

The gap between our "yes" and our "but" is not just an annoyed-plaintiff-in-a-boring-deposition problem, it's also a me problem. We live in a culture that's riddled with a "Yes, Lord ... but I've got way too much going on" syndrome. It's the spiritual version of saying "I'm here for it, Lord" while running a million miles an hour with a Frappuccino in one hand and a Target return in the other.

And listen, it doesn't take a psychologist to diagnose this syndrome—though, fun fact, I do have a psychology degree. Right next to my law degree. Both currently weeping under a pile of to-do lists and Chick-fil-A cups. (Bless my overeducated, underutilized heart.)

Consider this as my evidence for our "yes … but" culture.

1. *Yes*, we all agree that drinking water is good for us. *But* the carbonated soft drink industry was estimated at $122.34 billion in 2024.[1] (I love you, Diet Dr Pepper.)
2. *Yes*, managing our money and saving for retirement is important. *But* the average American has consumer debt of $105,000.[2]
3. *Yes*, studies warn that social media may lead to increased anxiety and depression. *But* Instagram has over 2 billion active users.[3]
4. *Yes*, the Bible instructs us to gather with other believers. *But* church membership is at a historic low in the Western world.[4]
5. *Yes*, prioritizing the people around us is important. *But* over 50 percent of Americans say there's not enough time in their day to complete all their tasks.[5]

This is more than a cultural issue; it's a faith issue. Jeff and Terra Mattson wrote an amazing book challenging Christians to shrink the gap between the values we preach and the way we actually live. That gap—or the integrity gap as they call it—is the distance between who we planned to be and who we actually are. We plan to say *yes* to the good things—especially being available for the God things—but then our *buts* tell the real story. (You're welcome for the deep theology right there.)

It reminds me of a story my mom recently told me.

There's a four-way stop near her house that drivers notoriously blow through. After years of watching near-misses, she was thrilled to see a police officer finally stationed there one afternoon. She walked right over and thanked him for enforcing the stop signs. It was far past time.

Less than twenty-four hours later, her canasta group rolled into the neighborhood, and one of her dear friends breezed right through that same stop sign—and got pulled over. Without hesitation, my mom rushed right across the street again. "Officer!" she said, "You can't ticket her—that sweet old lady is my friend!"

That dilemma is the crux of our integrity gap: championing obedience, doing the hard things, living interruptibly ... as long as it only applies to other people. When it comes to our lives? We've got spreadsheets, calendars (paper and Google versions), a vision board, and absolutely zero margin for detours—unless, of course, Jesus Himself sends the calendar invite.

We plan to say *yes* to the good things—especially being available for the God things—but then our *buts* tell the real story.

I've personally mastered the art of the polite Christian "yes ... but." Cloaked in my church lady smile, and sometimes even accessorized with Scripture, I remind God (and anyone else who'll listen) that my kids are still young-ish, my husband travels, someone else is way more qualified, our finances are limited, my faith sometimes wobbles, I'm ridiculously flawed and perpetually tired—and, honestly, why does it feel like I'm the only one getting roped into this stuff?

The pastor of my church, Libin Abraham, says it best: "God moves at the pace of your next yes."[6] The ones who don't miss it know that God's inviting us into His bigger purpose, but it starts with a "yes" to being interrupted from our own best-laid plans.

Here's the deal with living interruptibly—it sounds great until it actually costs me something. Like time. Or comfort. Or control. Or a clean house. Or my plan to binge *Beat Bobby Flay* in hopes of upping my crispy rice game.

Yet Jesus modeled interruptibility over and over as He was detoured by blind beggars, hemorrhaging women, short men in trees, and hungry crowds. I'm still looking for that occasion where He said, "Sorry about all this, but I've got sermon prep with John at 3:30. There's got to be someone with more margin who can help out."

The Yes That Almost Got Away

I'll never forget my super-spiritual response to the first time I sensed the Lord calling us to foster care. I was like, "Seriously Lord, us? We've got two kids, jobs, various commitments to our church, and a select sports schedule that would blow anyone's mind. Not to mention foster care is for super-religious people, like missionaries or people who play in the handbell choir or something. Surely, You don't mean us, Lord. We're not *those* kinds of Christians."

I was scared of foster care on every level—physically, emotionally, and spiritually.

It was one of the many times I've found myself caught between the "yes" and the "but."

- *Yes*, we believe Jesus loves every single one of His children and calls us to care for orphans, *but* we already have two kids of our own to raise.
- *Yes*, we know there are over 20,000 children in the foster care system in Texas, *but* we're just one family—what difference could we possibly make?
- *Yes*, we want to follow God's call, *but* foster care is a huge commitment, and let's be honest, not a lot of people around us are doing it.

I wish I was kidding, but those were my actual thoughts. Thankfully, despite a million arguably legitimate excuses, when the phone call came in the wee hours of the morning to take our very first placement, we gave a most reluctant yes to God.

A decade later, I can say I went into foster care scared of what it would do to our family, and I came out of foster care scared of who we would be if we had not done it.

It's not lost on me that God could have chosen any family for this story—yet it's humbling to realize He chose us. And if we had allowed our excuses to keep us from being interrupted, we would have missed the incredible gift of JB entirely.

Even so, the call to interruptibility took several forms over the years. It started with being **physically interruptible**. I was convinced this was the big one when we first got started in foster care. How were we ever going to balance another kiddo in the mix, especially a child who comes with Child Protective Services visits, court dates, and additional medical considerations? The physical demands of adding another child, especially a newborn, to our already overbooked lives was the biggest hurdle I thought we would face.

I remember people saying to us, "I don't know how you have time for this. We're maxed out with what we've already got on our plate."

And then right when we got a handle on the physical interruption of it, we began to feel the **emotional interruption**. When JB came to our house as a two-month-old little pumpkin, we assumed he would be with us for a very short time. But when weeks turned to months, and months turned to years, he was literally one of our family. We were all this little boy knew and, likewise, it felt like he was all we knew after such a long period of time. We loved him like our own and every time there was a court hearing that could potentially take him from our home, it was devastating to consider losing him.

People would say to us, "I could never do this because we would become too attached." (My snarky self always wanted to say, "Really? Not a problem here. We're cold as ice and totally not attached." Thankfully I kept my mouth shut.)

Just as we found our footing—learning to embrace the physical and emotional interruptions that came with the uncertainty of loving this precious little boy—along came a **spiritual interruption** I never saw coming. We desperately wanted to adopt JB, believing that it was the best possible outcome for his future. But every setback in his case was a reminder that stepping into God's calling often comes with a spiritual battle.

I have known Jesus for most of my life, but did I really believe God was for us? That He could do all things? If so, how was I supposed to reconcile my faith with the very real possibility that JB could be sent back to an unstable home? I had to decide if I actually believed what I'd always claimed. That God is good and kind and goes before us in all things.

I remember people commenting, "You must have a stronger faith than us to be able to walk this road." (I'll refrain from telling you what my snarky self wanted to say in response to this one.)

Make Breakfast and Don't Miss the Point

My husband, Mike, sent me a TED Talk the other day because our relationship is super spicy that way—exchanging steamy TED Talk texts at lunchtime. The speaker was Simon Sinek, and he was talking about corporate leadership and how the *most* successful leaders begin with their why. Our tendency (in business and otherwise) is to go straight to the how or even the what. We have the answers to what we sell or how we sell it, but not the why behind what we do (profit doesn't count, that's a result). Working from the what and how, he says, is working from the outside in. But starting with the why is working from the inside out and it makes all the difference between those who are successful and those who stall out.[7]

In a faith context, we can all agree that being available to serve people is critically important. We say yes to it—at least intellectually. God has plans for each of us that He designed before we took our first breath, and none of those happens if we're not willing to be interrupted. If the greatest commandment is to love God and love your neighbor, then being available is a no-brainer. You can call it living with availability, interruptibility, or having margin for how God wants to use us to minister to those around us. But somewhere between the "what" I am supposed to do and "how" I will make time to do it, the mission self-destructs. When we're working from the outside in, it gets lost in translation because we've forgotten our "why."

If the greatest commandment is to love God and love your neighbor, then being available is a no-brainer.

In the days after His resurrection, Jesus made cameos to His disciples (among others). During one particular drop-by to Peter and the disciples, Jesus helped them catch a boatload of fish and then made them breakfast. I feel like this may tell us all we need to know about Jesus' thoughts on interruptibility. If Jesus, a recently crucified man with a mission to save the world, has time to give fishing advice and then have breakfast with a few of His followers, what do we *not* have time for?

Yet after breakfast He had an interesting conversation with Peter, asking him a series of questions that went like this:

> "Peter, do you love Me?"
> "Yes, Lord."
> "Then feed My lambs."

And then a second time.

> "Peter, do you love Me?"
> "Yes, Lord."
> "Feed My sheep."

And then a third time.

> "Peter, do you love Me?"
> "Yes, Lord, You know all things; You know that I love You."
> "Feed My sheep."

There's a whole lot of commentary around this passage (see John 21:15–19) and how Jesus' asking three separate times is symbolic of the three times Peter denied Him. It's also Jesus' way of giving Peter the go-ahead to continue his ministry as a disciple. But the plain and simple message to Peter is also the same message for us: if we love Jesus, we've got to be interruptible and available to serve His people.

Our love for Jesus is the why behind our willingness to be interruptible.

It's the why behind our willingness to take care of those around us.

It's the why behind saying yes when our butt would rather say no.

What You Do Proves What You Believe

I don't share our foster care journey to imply we're getting it right and others are not. But when I think back to the reactions people had to us during that season, I realize they're the same excuses I *still* use every time God calls me out of my comfort zone—when He disrupts my plans and asks me to trust Him anyway.

The conversation goes something like this:

> "Do you love Me?"
> "Yes, Lord, but I'm maxed out with what's already on my plate."
> "Feed My sheep."
>
> "Do you love Me?
> "Yes, Lord, but I'm afraid I'll get too attached and it's going to leave a mark."
> "Feed My sheep."
>
> "Do you love Me?"
> "Yes, Lord, but You must have people with stronger faith who can do this hard thing."
> "Feed My sheep."

Simon Sinek said it well in his TED Talk: "What you do simply proves what you believe."[8] And that's where the real challenge lies—in the integrity gap between our "yes" and our "but."

Sometimes that means stepping into stories we'd rather ignore. Other times, it means going to places we've been trying to avoid. Sometimes it's big—foster care, job changes, mission trips. Other times, it's small—dropping off a meal, engaging a store clerk, or giving a little more generously than feels comfortable.

No matter what it looks like, it all boils down to the same decision: Will we be interruptible knowing it comes at a cost—physically, emotionally, and spiritually? Jesus' call to feed His sheep isn't hypothetical or metaphorical, it's literal.

Don't miss it: In a world where busyness is a badge of honor, *interruptibility* is our badge of love.

A Hole in Our Testimony

Samuel Langley was a well-funded, well-known figure in aviation in the early 1900s. Langley had all the resources: best engineers, funding from the War Department, and the *New York Times* following him for daily coverage. But his desire for public recognition overshadowed his passion for advancing flight. He was working from the outside in. Meanwhile, in Dayton, Ohio, Orville and Wilbur Wright had nothing but a bicycle shop and a vision. No press, no funding, just their firm belief the invention of air travel could change the world. They worked from the inside out.

The fact that you've no doubt heard of the Wright brothers but probably not heard of Samuel Langley is the headline here.

As Simon Sinek (our TED Talk dude) points out, most of us have a bicycle shop instead of a dream team. We don't have endless resources, time, recognition, or an audience documenting our every move. What we do have is what matters most—and it's our why. And if our why is to love Jesus, then we must be willing to be interrupted, to love His people—whether it's inconvenient, unnoticed, or even met with failure.

Like the gentleman in my deposition, we have one shot in this life to tell our story. If we refuse to be interrupted—clinging to comfort, schedules, or ambition—then we're basically wearing a mask with a cigarette hole in it. Going through the motions but accomplishing little. Don't be deceived, there may not be a court reporter transcribing our words, but our actions are the permanent record of our testimony.

Don't Miss It

- In a world where busyness is a badge of honor, interruptibility is our badge of love.
- If Jesus had time to cook breakfast for His friends after the cross, what are we too busy to do?
- Our love for Jesus is the why behind saying yes when our butt would rather say no.

Chapter 16

Tapback Trauma and Thirteen Hours of Compassion

I have a few strengths.

Come to think of it, I'll share a few of them with you right now. Seriously, it's no trouble.

I'm fairly patient (unless you give a 👍 to a text where I just poured out my heart. A little thing I call "tapback trauma.")

I don't take myself too seriously (except when my family argues that I'm not the funniest in the house. That's heresy).

I can stand on a stage and talk pretty good, most days (although maybe I just get asked because I'm more available than Ann Voskamp and Lisa Harper).

More often than not, I listen and obey the Lord when He asks me to do hard things.

And I have the perfect lime-to-onion ratio when making guacamole.

But I also have a gaping weakness. For instance, I never know how many *o*'s to use when spelling *lose* and *loose*—which feels like a *loosing* battle. Oh, and there's this little situation when it comes to my caretaking abilities. Or maybe I should say, my empathy as related to my caretaking abilities. My family could write their own book about this situation, to which I would respond with a 👍.

Here's the deal: When you're sick, I will take your temperature and dose you with Tylenol. I will take you to the doctor and pick up your prescriptions. I will bring you soup and sit by your side to watch movies. I'm willing to do all of this for approximately thirteen hours. After that, I'm gonna need you to man up.

Although it's taken me twenty years to realize I might have a slight compassion problem, admitting so feels like progress. Because it's been brought to my attention that dispensing Tylenol and soup is not sufficient proof of my mercies in the face of my family's endless complaining, bellyaching, and malingering.

A few years ago, *The Babylon Bee* hilariously posted a fake news story picturing a wife holding a cold pack on her husband's head with this headline: "'This Is the Worst Pain Any Human Has Ever Felt,' Man with Flu Tells Wife Who Pushed 3 Children Out of Body."[1]

I've never felt more seen.

When Mike and I were young parents and newly-ish married, his parents came to visit for the weekend. Kate was young and living out her terrible twos each day with excellence. Mike kept complaining that he had a headache and wasn't feeling great. We were out and about all weekend entertaining his parents, and between Kate's tantrums and Mike droning on and on about a headache—it was getting really old, really fast. At some point in the weekend, I had heard enough about Mike's mystery illness, and I spoke these fateful words: "Take a Benadryl and get over it."

We were in the process of moving into a new home, and a few days later I was painting the playroom when Mike came home early from work. He never comes home that early, so I wondered what was going on (and was secretly thinking, *It'd better not be that darn headache again*). He said that he felt numbness in his left arm and wondered if he might be having a stroke.

Now he had my attention, so we rushed to the emergency room, and they ran all kinds of tests and eventually diagnosed him with a migraine and sent us home. That restarted the clock, and I'll have you know that I gladly gave him Tylenol, soup, and another thirteen hours of compassion. But he seemed to be getting worse, and a few nights later he woke me up in the middle of the night and started asking questions that didn't make sense. He was confused about where he was, who I was, and what year it was. (I, too, was confused and had my own question as to why this mysterious illness was lasting so long, but thankfully this time I kept my uncompassionate mouth shut.)

Fast-forward through many ER visits, countless specialists, two hospitals, and many weeks in ICU, we finally received a diagnosis. Mike had meningitis and encephalitis. As one doctor described it to me, meningitis will make you very sick, but encephalitis will kill you. Encephalitis, if you aren't familiar with it (which I pray you are not) is a swelling of the brain that disrupts brain function. And just FYI, best practices for treating encephalitis do not include suggesting one take a Benadryl and suck it up.

My apologies.

Mike spent several weeks in and out of the ICU and didn't return to work for months. I'll never forget the words of his infectious disease doctor when they finally discharged him. This doctor, a well-known expert in his field, told us that in all his years of practice, he had never seen a case of meningitis combined with encephalitis where the patient walked away with no residual effects—but Mike did. As one of my good friends says, this falls in the miracle category.

Upstream Faith for Downstream Miracles

During the time Mike was in the ICU battling encephalitis, some of our dear friends from our Sunday school class, the Dodgens, were just two floors above us in the same hospital, celebrating the birth of their baby girl, Abby. Each day many of our church friends would come to the hospital to meet precious Abby and then come down to the ICU waiting room to pray for Mike as he fought for his life. It was a surreal mix of joy and heartache; a reminder of how life can hold both unspeakable beauty and deep pain in the shortest of distances.

A few days after Abby's birth, her parents received the heartbreaking and unexpected news: she had a congenital heart defect—one that would ultimately claim her precious life. Mike told the doctors, in no uncertain terms, that approval or not, he would be leaving the hospital to attend her funeral. When the day arrived, Mike was there. Barely able to walk, pale, weak, and far from healed, he showed up. No one could have imagined that our sweet Sunday school class would gather at a funeral for a baby whose life was taken far too soon, while Mike—who had been critically ill—was spared.

One story ended with miraculous healing—clear and immediate, right before our eyes. While the other required an upstream faith, the kind of faith that trusts God is at work, even in the face of tragedy, in ways we cannot yet see or fully understand.

This kind of faith played out when the Israelites were heading to the Promised Land and found themselves facing the Jordan River. At first glance, we might think, *What's the big deal? Just cross the river.* But it wasn't just any river; it was harvest season, and the water was at its highest, overflowing its banks. A daunting obstacle, to say the least.

Then, just as the priests followed God's instructions and dipped their toes into the rushing water, something incredible happened. The water stopped flowing. It instantly receded, clearing a path for the Israelites to cross. It was a miracle of "biblical proportions."

Although most of us are probably familiar with this story, here's the part that often gets overlooked. It's a seemingly small, almost parenthetical detail in Joshua 3:16 that holds profound significance:

> The water from upstream stopped flowing. It piled up in a heap a great distance away, at a town called Adam.

Adam, just a distant, unremarkable town. Nothing extraordinary, at first glance. But consider this: long before the Israelites faced the overflowing Jordan River, blocking their path to the very place God had promised them—God was already at work. Twenty miles away, upstream in Adam, He had already dammed the waters. The solution was in motion before the Israelites even knew the problem existed.

That's the beauty of an upstream God. He is always at work, has already set miracles in motion—long before we notice the problem or understand how it will all unfold. You may not feel it yet; you may not see the evidence. But somewhere upstream, God is at work. You can trust the hand of God who works all things for our good (see Rom. 8:28). Because if it isn't good, then it isn't finished. That's the promise of an upstream faith.

Somewhere upstream, God is at work.

But admittedly this comes from the perspective of the Israelites. The ones standing at the water's edge, desperately waiting for a miraculous parting. The ones who walked on dry ground and safely reached the other side.

What about the Adam-ites? The inhabitants of the town likely had no idea what was unfolding when the waters began spilling over in epic proportions. To them, it must have looked like a disaster—a catastrophic event with no explanation. Why would God let this happen? If He controls all things, why wouldn't He stop the rise of these waters? Yet, what the Adam-ites couldn't see was that, downstream, God was orchestrating a miracle that would change the course of human history forever. Their chaos was God's calculated choreography, sparing an entire nation of Israelites.

Here's the juxtaposition (a word I've been dying to use): Sometimes we have the advantage of being an Israelite, standing on the shore, watching the waters part, and witnessing the miracle unfold before our eyes. Those are amazing moments, especially after upstream faith moments of trusting God in places we cannot see.

At other times, we're Adam-ites, stuck upstream in the chaos, watching the waters rise and wondering why the God who can do anything, heal anyone, move any mountain is silent. But just because the downstream miracle is hidden from our view—just because it seems unnecessarily chaotic—doesn't make it any less miraculous. Because today's chaos and confusion often set the stage for tomorrow's miracle.

The Intersection of Miracles and Mission

I think we've established that my caretaking abilities are subpar. I'm praying yours are stronger. Honestly, it wouldn't take much. But here's an admittedly strange question we should ask ourselves: How well are we caretaking the miracles in our lives?

Louie Giglio makes the point that miracles are always attached to the mission of Jesus.[2] That thread runs straight through the Gospels. Jesus didn't heal just for the spectacle or simply for convenience—He did it to draw hearts back to the Father. Every miracle was a spotlight pointing to His power, His love, and His invitation into something eternal.

And when the blind saw, when the lame walked, when the dead rose—yes, those individuals were transformed—but so were the ones standing nearby. Miracle watchers became Jesus followers. Bystanders became believers.

And isn't that the story of the gospel itself? God's power. His sovereignty. His relentless pursuit of our hearts. The whole of redemptive history is one miracle after another, threaded together by a God who brings hope where there otherwise is none.

Today's chaos and confusion often set the stage for tomorrow's miracle.

When the Israelites crossed the Jordan, their first instinct wasn't to question or explain away the miracle. They didn't argue about the physics of a dried-up riverbed or wonder if the timing had just been lucky. No—they knew God had moved. And they responded not with doubt but with remembrance. Joshua had them gather stones and stack them high as a memorial, a visible, undeniable reminder of what God had done. So that generations to come would know. So they'd never forget His faithfulness.

We are living in the overflow of miracles every single day. We wake up to oxygen in our lungs, birds chirping in our ears, sunrises we didn't earn and sunsets we can't miss. When was the last time we built a memorial for those? When did we gather stones to say, "We will not forget. We refuse to let this go unacknowledged, unnoticed, uncelebrated."

Every miracle, big or small, is an invitation to make Jesus known. He doesn't heal just to make us whole—He heals to make us His. He doesn't provide just to fill a need—He provides to fill us with Himself. Miracles are not isolated blessings; they are gospel moments. And we are their caretakers.

I've seen it up close in my own home. When God gave Mike more earth days, he didn't waste them. Mike stopped traveling so much. Worked fewer hours. Said yes to coaching high school softball, not just for the sport but for the souls of teenage girls who needed encouragement, leadership, and the example of an unwavering love of Jesus. He opened his Bible more. Prayed longer. Chose to be present with his family. His miracle didn't just bless him—it refueled his mission.

And then there's the story of the Dodgens and baby Abby. They didn't get the earthly miracle we begged God for. But somehow—graciously, courageously—they've shown us what it looks like to carry the mission of Jesus *without* the miracle. They've clung to faith even when their hearts were broken, walking a path no parent ever wants to walk. Their marriage has been a testimony of a God-centered life. Their sons are being raised in truth and hope. And I believe with everything in me that one day soon heaven will tell the full story—of lives changed, hearts softened, of faith ignited, of people drawn to Jesus by the quiet, steady strength of a family who chose faith even without the miracle.

Both stories are attached to the mission of Jesus. One shows what God can do when the waters part. The other shows what He can do when they don't.

Louie Giglio says the key to stewarding miracles—whether we receive them or not—is to "raise the volume of the gospel above the narrative of the circumstance."[3] The headline isn't the circumstance; the headline is the gospel. And the Dodgens have lived this well.

Palm Readers

When Mike was recovering from meningitis and encephalitis, the neurologist came in each day to check his progress. Most days his best medical advice for patients with brain inflammation was this: "Take a Benadryl and get over it." (Kidding, sadly.) But he did have a simple but telling way of checking Mike's progress. Using just his finger, he'd trace a question mark, a shape, or even a random word on Mike's palm. Sometimes Mike would recognize the writing immediately—a relief that his healing was progressing. Other times, Mike would look visibly concerned, struggling to make sense of what the doctor was tracing.

Is it possible the Great Physician is doing the same with us?

That even now, God is gently tracing His plans into the palm of our hands? Maybe we recognize His work—we're beginning to see the healing, the provision, and the miracle He's bringing into focus. Or maybe, like Mike on those harder days, we feel confused, squinting and wondering what He's writing in the midst of the unexpected diagnosis, parenting struggles, or professional setbacks.

Here's the hope we can hold on to—just because we can't recognize His writing doesn't mean He isn't at work.

Let the town of Adam remind us that God is always working upstream—long before we realize we even need a miracle. Let the Dodgens remind us that faith isn't about the outcome; it's about trusting the Author. And let my pitiful caretaking abilities remind us that not every problem can be resolved in thirteen hours or less.

So with palms open, let's trust the One who writes miracles into the details of our lives. Because whether it's immediately recognizable or not, His work is good.

Don't Miss It

- Sometimes faith means carrying the mission of Jesus, even when the waters didn't part.
- Every miracle, big or small, is an invitation to make Jesus known.
- You don't have to recognize what He's writing to trust that His hand is at work. (So, in the meantime, take a Benadryl and wait it out.)

Chapter 17

Roller Coasters, Tang, and Benchwarmers

I hold my parents wholly responsible for raising me and my brothers to be the least cultured people you've ever met. I've scoured my memory banks for even one shred of cultured evidence in order to negate this bold assertion.

I've got nothing.

My case for "unculturedness" (which I'm pretty sure isn't a word, and yet ... here we are) is airtight. I even asked Google what makes someone cultured, hoping for a technicality to cling to. Apparently, it involves being well-versed in history, cuisine, art, diverse cultures, and—this part feels personal—having good manners.

Let's unpack this a bit.

Cuisine

Have you ever been served half a peach filled with mayonnaise, grated cheese, and topped with a cherry?

Have you eaten a beef product generously named "Swiss steak" that looks like it went twelve rounds with a can of stewed tomatoes—and lost?

Have you experienced a carrot and grape salad conceived in a Jell-O mold? And then washed all of this down with a tall glass of Tang?

Well, I have. And it was a crime against humanity.

To be fair, my mom is a phenomenal cook. But I grew up in the '70s, when menu planning was more of a flip through the red-and-white-checkered *Better Homes and Gardens* cookbook rather than a sophisticated browse through *Bon Appétit*. It was a decade equally unkind to palates and perms.

History

Comedian Nate Bargatze once said he doesn't know much about history, and when he watched the movie *Pearl Harbor*, he was as surprised as the US Navy. I've never felt more seen. That basically sums up my history knowledge. I have no idea who fought in what war or what decade or even what country. What were they mad about to even start a war? Got me.

It's bad enough that I don't know for myself, but my poor kids ... I once told them that Texas won the Alamo. I was serious. I even argued with Mike when he tried to correct me. I learned my lesson, though—to this day whenever my kids ask me a history question, I caution them, saying, "Remember the Alamo."

Culture

As I've mentioned, we grew up in El Paso, Texas—a border town steeped in Mexican culture—which you'd think would've bumped up our sophistication score. But it turns out my brothers' frequent trips across the border in high school had more to do with the drinking age than any cultural curiosity.

Their favorite spot was called Fred's, a place where teenage patrons (that's being generous) would sit in a circle, hold hands, and pay for an employee to attach a battery charger to one end of the group, sending a current through the entire circle. Shocking, I know. And yet you know what's not shocking about this story? My brothers are still uncultured.

Travel

My parents were gracious enough to take us on several family vacations. They also sent us on every church trip possible. I'm grateful for this, though, in true "no good deed goes unpunished" style, as teenagers, my brothers once called home complaining that the youth leaders were making them hang out in a graveyard all day. Turns out it was Arlington National Cemetery. #Uncultured

The great thing about those church trips is that they bait-and-switched us into missions work with the promise of hitting an amusement park on the way home. I have priceless memories from those blazing hot park days: cold nachos with decades-old processed cheese, a forty-dollar T-shirt with my boyfriend's face airbrushed on it (why?), and sunburns so bad that thirty-five years later, I'm personally funding my dermatologist's lake house (you're welcome, Dr. Parker).

But culture or no culture, here's one thing you need to know about me: I don't do roller coasters. I hate heights, I despise that stomach-drop sensation, and frankly, I prefer to keep my innards in their God-given configuration. Instead, I proudly serve as the designated cell phone and backpack holder at amusement parks. Yes, it's one of the lesser-known spiritual gifts.

The key to this role is finding a sliver of bench near the ride's entrance—usually between the stroller parking lot and the "You Must Be This Tall to Ride" sign. That's where I settle in for the long haul (picture camping out for Black Friday at Best Buy) of people-watching and guarding the valuables.

There's a whole bench ecosystem out there in the amusement park world: On one end, exhausted grandparents silently questioning every "This'll be fun!" decision they've ever made. In the middle, a frazzled mom peeling string cheese for a toddler in a stroller while explaining to her six-year-old son why he can't ride the Tower of Terror with dad. Somewhere off to the side, there's "that guy" chain-smoking like it's 1972, blowing smoke in your face while scrolling Autotrader for a used Camaro.

Then there's me. Cautiously manning the cell phones and backpacks while everyone else is on the ride of their life.

The Benched Life

The bench is where dreams go to die. Okay, fine—maybe that's too strong a statement. But the bench is safe. Predictable. It's where we park ourselves when the high highs and the low lows feel a little too risky to stomach. The bench doesn't ask too much—you just hold everyone's stuff and wait, comfortably out of the action, nestled between string cheese and secondhand smoke.

I've sat there many, many times. And not just at amusement parks.

It's happened when I've been too embarrassed to mention my faith to a new friend, or let fear talk me out of pursuing something God clearly put on my heart, or even ignored the prompting to go on the missions trip (especially when there wasn't an amusement park promised). Sometimes I've stayed on the bench because it was easier. Sometimes because I didn't feel qualified. Sometimes because I let someone else's doubt drown out God's voice. And sometimes because Netflix had released a new show called *Inventing Anna*.

Whatever the reason, the result was the same: I missed out. Not on my salvation, not on God's unconditional love for me—but on the kind of adventure that stretches my faith, deepens my trust, and leaves me running off the ride breathless, wide-eyed, and yelling, "Let's do that again."

When we get off the bench and buckle in, we open the door to the incredible, unpredictable stories only God can write—and thankfully, at times I've had a front-row seat to watching Him use those highs and lows to do His most significant work in my own life.

When we choose comfort over obedience and safety over faith, we miss the thrill of the story God's waiting to write through our lives.

Because without the low of feeling totally unequipped when a foster baby arrived at our home with nothing but a diaper, I would have missed the high of God moving mountains to weave a miraculous adoption story into our family.

Without the low of the sting of betrayal after pouring my heart into a ministry, I would have missed the high of God using that pain as a training ground for a deeper, wider calling.

Without the low of the uncertainty of a learning difference diagnosis for my child, I would have missed the high of watching him grow into the hardest worker and kindest soul I know.

Without the low of not knowing how we would pay the hospital bills and the mortgage, we would have missed the high of watching God's generosity show up the moment we needed it most.

Without the low of loving someone who can't tear his eyes away from the game playing on the TV above my head on date night, I would miss the high of learning that grace and laughter keep a marriage strong.

The highs and lows aren't just for roller coasters; they're part of the journey God calls each of us to walk. And just like me, parked on that bench year after year, watching everyone else take the ride of a lifetime, when we choose comfort over obedience and safety over faith, we miss the thrill of the story God's waiting to write through our lives.

Arise from the Cell Phones

Gosh, I love the story of Jonah. He's the poster child for "not my circus, not my monkeys." He hated the Ninevites and got real mad when he was minding his own business and God asked him to get involved by warning them of their impending doom. In no way, shape, or form was Jonah a friend to those people, and he wanted no part in their rescue. But God was pretty blunt: get over yourself and do what's right. No gentle nudges here; God told him to "arise" not once, but twice. Arise and go to Nineveh—that was the unwanted calling on Jonah's life (Jon. 1:2; 3:2 ESV).

The literal definition of *arise* is "to get up or stand up," and it can also mean "to begin to occur or exist."[1] I love how both definitions line up with the way God, biblically speaking, tells His people to get up and move toward a life that exists within His greater purposes. It's not just about physically standing—it's a call to action. A call to step into something new.

Throughout the Bible, the words *arise* or *rise* don't just signal a shift in posture—but a shift in purpose. God tells people to "arise" right when He's about to do something big:

- God told Abram to "arise" and walk through the land that he would soon inherit. (Gen. 13:17 ESV)
- God told Joseph, "Rise, take the child and his mother" and flee to Egypt so Herod wouldn't kill Him. (Matt. 2:13 ESV)
- Isaiah told the Israelites, "Arise, shine, for your light has come," speaking of God's promise to bring their Redeemer. (Isa. 60:1 ESV)
- Jesus told a paralyzed man, "Arise, take up your bed, and go to your house," giving a once forgotten man a miraculous view of God's power. (Matt. 9:6 NKJV)

Don't miss that last example: Here's a guy who was probably resigned to a life that felt purposeless. Hopeless. Totally benched. Yet with one word—*arise*—Jesus invited him into a whole new way of life. This was an invitation to do what is hard, hopeless, uncomfortable—to stand when standing was impossible, walk when walking was inconceivable.

Jesus uses situations that once felt burdensome, unsolvable, or downright terrifying to become the very testimonies that point others to Him. But notice how these "arise" examples above are all followed by a verb. A call to action. Yes, the call to arise starts with a willingness to stand up—it's making the decision to get off the bench and step into the opportunities Jesus puts in front of us, especially the ones that are hard and sometimes even undesirable in the moment.

The Bible is full of people who got off the bench when they were called to "arise":

- Noah's arise moment meant building a boat that saved his family and every generation that followed.
- Moses's arise moment meant leading an exodus that would free a nation and deliver God's law to the world.
- Joseph's arise moment meant storing grain that would preserve his family and the entire future of Israel.
- Rahab's arise moment meant hiding spies, saving her family, and helping God's people enter the Promised Land.

- Mary's arise moment meant saying yes to carrying the Messiah and ultimately offering hope to a broken world.
- Jesus' arise moment (quite literally) meant conquering sin and death so we could live forever.

Which brings us right back to the benchwarmers.

When we sit too long on the bench—holding the backpacks, managing the schedules, busying ourselves into burnout all in the name of keeping the chaos at bay—it's easy to convince ourselves that we have no other option. Or maybe we've believed the lie that our best days, our highest calling, or our greatest usefulness for the kingdom is for another time—when life isn't so complicated. A lot of us have convinced ourselves that our best kingdom-difference moments are behind us. That someone else is now better suited for the ride.

The bench is fine for a moment. We all need rest. But if we're not careful, we settle for spectating instead of participating. Let me say that again—if we're not careful, we settle for spectating instead of participating. We talk ourselves out of the story God is writing because we've gotten really comfortable sitting and watching others take the ride.

When Mike edited this chapter, he insisted I include a sports analogy (refer back to that date-night TV situation for context). He said professional athletes don't choose to sit on the bench. They want in. When their name is called, they can't get off the bench fast enough. No one hears the coach say, "You're up—we need you," and then shrugs it off, deciding they'd rather hang out on the bench. That's not how the game works. And it's definitely not how God works. The God of the universe has called your number—why would you possibly bench yourself?

God is not calling you to stay benched, managing everyone else's stuff, while this brief life passes you by.

So arise, and—

Start the ministry.

Say yes to the foster placement.

Teach preschool Sunday school.

Write the book.

Book the flight.

Call your mom.

Show up at counseling.

Say you're sorry.

Share your faith.

I don't know what your "arise" moment looks like, but I do know that God is not calling you to stay benched, managing everyone else's stuff, while this brief life passes you by. He's inviting you to arise and take your place in His-story. Not because you feel prepared, confident, and you've got it all figured out ... but because He does.

Yes to the Roller Coaster, No to Mayonnaise Peaches

I probably owe my parents an apology for blaming them for our lack of culture—in print, no less—especially since my family is leaving tomorrow to meet them in Rome for a vacation. So while I'm sorry for the lack-of-culture accusations, I will not apologize for calling out the Tang and mayonnaise peaches.

Yet beyond the questionable cuisine and my complete historical ignorance, I'll always be thankful for what my parents did teach us—that is to get on the ride. Say yes when every part of you wants to say no. Show up when no one else thinks it matters. Serve selflessly even when it feels like it won't make a dent. Step out when you think you'll likely fail. And arise—stand up—even when the safest spot is the bench, clutching someone else's backpack and praying you don't die an early death from secondhand smoke.

My parents modeled a faith that wasn't content with the sidelines—they got messy, made mistakes, and over and over we watched them buckle up for a tumultuous ride. They didn't just talk about faith; they lived it, showing us how to wrestle through the tension of wanting to cling to the bench that feels safe but knowing that's not where God does His best work.

So I'll keep working to stay off the bench—spiritually speaking. (Roller coasters are still a hard no.) I'll keep saying yes to the scary asks more often than not. I'll take the lows that leave me breathless and lean into the highs that leave me grateful. Because I don't want to look back on a life of spray-painted T-shirts and bad sunburns only to realize I missed the ride of a lifetime.

Don't Miss It

- God calls us to participate, not spectate.
- Sometimes "figuring it all out" begins with a simple yes.
- Don't settle for a life of spray-painted T-shirts and bad sunburns only to realize you missed out on the ride of a lifetime.

Chapter 18

Your Own Personal Mount Rushmore

(Chapter title intended to be hummed to the Depeche Mode tune)

I don't really have a bucket list, but if I did, it would include a trip to Mount Rushmore.

Okay, to be fully transparent, I only said Mount Rushmore because it sounds more respectable than admitting that I'm dying to be on QVC. Yes, I would give my left kidney to be a host on that show for a day (or even an ovary, but they might be too old and shriveled and I'm not sure if that's good leverage). It's a deeply complicated relationship I have with that network, beginning with having no idea what their acronym stands for.

Questionable Value Channel
Quilts Vacuums Caftans (to be clear, I support all three)
Quit Voluntarily, Cynthia

It's anyone's guess.

But the moment I flip to that channel I instantly feel a few decades younger. There's something about those sweet Midwestern grandmas calling in to talk about their collectible nutcrackers and ordering prime rib for the Christmas table that heals me. And, yes, QVC sells food. If you've never seen a thirteen-pound Junior's cheesecake being sold with the seriousness of a NASA launch countdown, I'm genuinely sorry for your misfortune.

Now if all the QVC stars align, you might also get the chance to purchase the TSV (Today's Special Value—please keep up) with free shipping—which is a huge value because cheesecake is dense, obviously.

Now, admittedly, there have been times when even I start off scoffing at that movable indoor herb garden shaped like a panda—but four minutes into that demonstration and a "last call" warning, and I'm suddenly running around looking for a credit card like I'm in the middle of a hostage negotiation.

Now let me try to answer a few questions you may have about my QVC "situation":

Do I have a "Qcard"?

I do not.

Am I contemplating getting one?

Obviously—because one day I'll be in a home and my kids are mean and I'm pretty sure they will try to keep me from the very things I need the most, like Mrs Prindables caramel apples and turtle figurines for the garden I might one day plant. The Qcard may be my only lifeline.

Do I have a favorite host?

Yes, Dave, whom I like to call "Uncle Dave" because at this point he's basically family. I'm determined to get on a plane to go tour QVC one day and meet Uncle Dave. Oh, and I may have been overheard telling Mike recently how proud I am of Uncle Dave's weight loss—and I meant it. That man could sell me a reversible rain poncho in the middle of the Sahara, and I'd not only buy it, I'd wear it, commend him on the moisture-locking technology, and ask if there's an option to get another one in leopard print. (And unlike my kids, he'd say yes and be happy for me.)

Blowing Things Up, Not Blowing Things Off

Second to QVC (and I mean a far, far second) on my bucket list is a trip to Mount Rushmore. If all goes as planned, one day I will march on up there with my battery-heated Sherpa hoodie and get a firsthand look at the craftsmanship that went into that massive iconic sculpture.

For those of us not as familiar with Mount Rushmore as we are with QVC, it originated as an idea by Doane Robinson to attract tourists to South Dakota. The head sculptor, Gutzon Borglum, convinced the decision-makers to carve something that would convey the larger meaning of America on the mountain—hence, the faces of George Washington, Thomas Jefferson, Abraham Lincoln, and Teddy Roosevelt.[1]

Borglum and his team had photographs and paintings of the four presidents that guided them in the sculpting process to ensure the details and proportions were correct. Fun fact: apparently 90 percent of the carving required the use of dynamite to remove large portions of the mountain. After that, they used a process called honeycombing where they drilled closely spaced holes into the granite to weaken it so they could remove rock, little by little, a few inches at a time, transforming the mountain into a masterpiece. Fourteen years and a million dollars later, Mount Rushmore was completed in 1941.[2]

I was reminded how sometimes our lives also need dynamite-sized actions: committing to heal our marriage, addressing the addiction, or reprioritizing our mental or physical health. But other times transformation happens in the slow, steady work—loving people when it's hard, choosing forgiveness, living interruptibly, giving generously, and showing up when it's inconvenient. Because a masterpiece is never carved in a single explosion; it's shaped by a thousand small, faithful steps.

So it was with Mount Rushmore. So it is with us.

Transformation often happens in the slow, steady work—loving people when it's hard, choosing forgiveness, living interruptibly, and showing up when it's inconvenient.

 Slow Carving, Big Impact

I'm guessing the early days of Mount Rushmore didn't look very impressive. People probably walked by and hardly noticed the hard work being done. Yet over time, what seemed infinitely small became a showpiece highlighting the faces of American presidents. Similarly, most times the little things of faith start off small and unimpressive. But then, after days and months and even years of carving away faithfully, our lives begin to take shape and the face of our beautiful Savior begins to emerge more and more clearly.

Dallas Willard is one of my favorite authors and theologians. He has a way of challenging people to step up and actually do the things that set our faith apart. It's tough to pick just one Dallas Willard quote, but this one is on my Mount Rushmore of great quotes.

> The general human failing is to want what is right and important, but at the same time not to commit to the kind of life that will produce the action we know to be right and the condition we want to enjoy.[3]

As you reflect on what really matters in the chapters of this book, I doubt any of this came as a brand-new revelation. You didn't read the chapter on gratitude and think, *Wow, this girl has figured it out. I truly never saw it coming that gratitude actually mattered.*

Of course not. You've heard it before—whether in sermons, in Scripture, or in conversations with wise friends. We know what's good, true, and right. But as Dallas Willard wisely pointed out, knowing isn't the same as doing. We want lives that matter for eternity, but that kind of life is built in the small, ordinary moments that often feel anything but significant. It's the stuff we tend to overlook, brushing past it in our busyness—until one day, life is humming along, we're flipping over to see what's on QVC, and we begin wondering, *How'd I miss that?*

Mount Rushmore is the perfect example. Although Doane Robinson is credited as the visionary for this famous national landmark, without years of carving, chiseling, and refining by hundreds of workers, it would have remained just an idea. The same is true for us. Love, kindness, courage—none of it changes lives if we're content just using the words. Jesus, the ultimate visionary, laid out the blueprint for an abundant life—but He also lived it. We're called to do the same. Transformation only comes when we pick up the chisel and day by day choose to carve Jesus' teachings into the nuances of our everyday life.

The Faces That Shape Us

Recently while I was interviewing Mark Batterson on my podcast, I noticed four prominent pictures hanging on the wall behind his desk. He told me they were his own Mount Rushmore. The pictures were of Albert Einstein, Teddy Roosevelt, George Washington Carver, and John Muir. These people remind him daily to live an inspired life.

I love this idea of having our own personal Mount Rushmore. I'm curious, who is on your Mount Rushmore? What people, memories, or places remind you that piece by piece you have the opportunity to carve out a life of great significance?

It may not be historic figures who have shaped American history or famous names who dominate headlines. It's almost certainly not TikTok stars with viral reels or professional athletes who've perfected their game. In all likelihood, it's the unsung heroes who have consistently and quietly lived out their calling day in and day out. It's people faithfully chiseling away—tiny piece by piece—their small portion of the larger portrait of Christ.

As I've been thinking about my own Mount Rushmore lately, I've found it hard to narrow down the people who have etched a lasting place in my soul. Truthfully, this entire book is a narrative of the little moments, big misses, and story after story of dear friends and family members who have demonstrated a life filled with the things that really matter.

But if I were to follow Mark Batterson's lead and put my own personal Mount Rushmore on the wall behind my desk, I would start by framing these four pictures:

1. **Peggy Powell.** An older woman who could have easily believed her best days were behind her. But the moment she heard about my friend going to prison, she stepped in the gap with a steady determination. She earns a place on my Mount Rushmore wall for the quiet faithfulness it takes to write a letter every single day—for almost a decade. No, it didn't come with applause or medals. But Peggy saw what I often miss: how something as ordinary as a pencil and a stamp

can bring the hope of Jesus to those who desperately need it.

2. **The Wright brothers.** Two men with no credentials, no funding, and no public platform—just a bicycle shop and a relentless belief that something bigger was possible. They are on my Mount Rushmore wall for their behind-the-scenes grit, doing the hard work that others won't, and knowing that changing history doesn't always come with big headlines. Their picture reminds me that when your mission is destined to change the world, you only need a bike shop—not a dream team (or platform, book deal, audience, seminary degree, or [fill in the blank]).
3. **A picture of my house** would also make my Mount Rushmore wall—not because of its fantastic landscaping (of which there is none), designer paint colors, or hardwood floors. But because it reminds me that every routine, often unnoticed decision I make is laying the foundation for the kind of life I'm building. Each choice to live interruptible, to love without conditions, to forgive when the grudge feels justified—those are the bricks and mortar of a home I actually want to live in. Because I remember living in a different kind of house—one formed by bitterness, pride, self-preservation, and comparison. I know what

it's like to live in that kind of house, and I won't be going back.

4. **Dylan Becker** holds the final spot on my Mount Rushmore wall—a reminder to live each day like it matters, because it does. I haven't mentioned Dylan before now because I just met him recently. He's in his midforties, married with two young kids, and nineteen months into a terminal cancer diagnosis that gave him a maximum of thirty-six months to live. When he was first diagnosed, Dylan asked about his prognosis. The doctors told him they don't like to talk about time frames. Funny enough, neither do we. But Dylan knows his earthly game is winding down—and instead of seeing it as a death sentence, it's been an invitation to really live.

In the months since his diagnosis, Dylan has fixed his gaze on Jesus, poured into his family, and helped others live on mission—now, not later. The things that used to feel important have faded. He's using every day to be a better father, friend, and follower of Jesus. Back in his college days, he played football at the University of Texas for legendary Coach Mack Brown. Coach Brown said that when it comes to priorities, faith and family come before everything else. Because when the lights go out and the crowd is gone, the people you need standing by your side the most are Jesus and your family. Dylan gets that now in a way most of us do not.

He's not waiting for a perfect moment or clean bill of health to make his life count. He's doing it now—with all he has, while he has it, and with Jesus firmly at the center of it all.

Transformation only comes when we pick up the chisel and day by day choose to carve Jesus' teaching into the nuances of our everyday life.

A Spiritual Earpiece of Sorts

I refuse to wrap up this book with everyone worrying about the devastating reality that my QVC dreams will likely never materialize. I'm a realist and have accepted the harsh truth that I'll probably never get to sell QVC's two-person inflatable heated hot tub while wearing their nonskid safety-sole slippers. Even so, the one part of the QVC experience that most intrigues me has always been that earpiece the hosts wear, giving the producer a direct line of communication during the show.

My cousin David (literally my cousin, not "Uncle Dave") was once on QVC selling toys and said that earpiece feeds you real-time updates like, "Sales are up when you say 'collectible,' but stop saying 'educational,' for the love of all that's good. And don't even think about mentioning batteries aren't included unless you're going to remind Nonnie that her precious grandkids are addicted to their phones." I can't help but think how I would thrive under those conditions—practical reminders on what resonates with people with warnings to stay away from heinous words like *moist*, *lover*, and *probes*.

What a game changer to have someone who knows the bigger picture, constantly weighing in on what matters, what's working, and what's not. I guess it wouldn't be that outlandish to think of Jesus as our own QVC earpiece (another little theological gem you won't hear in any reputable seminary). But we have direct access to the very One who commands the rising sun and steadies the earth on its invisible axis. He breathes galaxies into place and hurls stars into the night with absolute precision and purpose. He's producing all of life and eternity while whispering in our ear, "Keep trying. Don't stop. Show grace. Bite your tongue. Live interruptibly, do the hard things, and remember this is not your home."

Yet somewhere in the middle of climbing professional ladders, sitting in car pool, and figuring out gluten-free snacks for next week's soccer game, perspective fades. Life gets loud. And one day you wake up and realize you could write an entire book filled with stories of all the times you've wondered, *How'd I miss that?*

Right now, in this very moment, Jesus is offering us critical reminders that our days count and that even the smallest acts—those mustard seed moments—carry eternal weight. He's showing us how slow, steady chiseling away at the mountain isn't wasted effort but our part in His greater masterpiece.

So, take it from a friend who refuses to let you walk around with spinach in your teeth—life is short, but eternity is long. It's the little things that make a big kingdom difference. Don't miss it.

Don't Miss It

- A masterpiece is never carved in a single explosion; it's shaped by thousands of tiny acts of obedience.
- Don't confuse your small act with small impact.
- Live each day for Jesus with the kind of urgency QVC uses to sell cheesecake—like someone's eternity depends on it.

Acknowledgments

My very favorite daughter, Kate, recently came back from vacation cackling about a restaurant where the waitstaff *throws* dinner rolls at you. Not in a panicked, "Duck and cover!" kind of way but more of an "Incoming!"—with a side of butter. It got the job done, made people laugh, and somehow turned a flying carbohydrate into a memorable experience.

Of course, Kate loved it—mostly because she's athletic enough to catch airborne bread without flinching. I, on the other hand, would've taken three rolls to the head, sat there blinking in confusion, and muttered, "How'd I miss that?" before kindly asking Mike to run interference.

I want to start by thanking you—**yes, you reader**—for showing up to the literary version of that restaurant. This book is me tossing rolls across the room and hoping you catch what you need. My prayer is that you received the substance you came for, but in a way that also made you laugh. I'm a firm believer that life is full of unexpected, hard-to-digest moments—and that they go down a little easier with Jesus, humor ... and carbs. Given the choice between messy life lessons delivered in a tidy breadbasket or hurled with humor across a crowded room, let's always pick the latter.

Like most big projects, this one didn't happen alone. So, to stay on theme, I'm going to have you picture me standing in the middle of the room, arms full of warm, buttery bread, hurling thank-you rolls at some of my favorite people:

My Family—You is kind. You is patient. You is glad this book is done. *Same.*

Mike, thank you for editing my words, censoring the inappropriate ones, and loving me with all my quirks—like hating to hold hands and complaining about sharing small hotel bathrooms.

Kate, thanks for being ridiculously funny and thoughtful and for talking to me in the car when all the boys say their day was "fine" and then go silent.

Brett, thank you for your deep wisdom, often disguised as sarcasm and one-liners, and for letting me throw you into a spotlight you'd never voluntarily step into.

And JB, thank you for not making me play make-believe games anymore and for rounding out our family in the most perfectly unique way.

Wednesday Lunch Crew, Besties, Raising Boys, Ladies Who Lunch, ABC, Stephanie, Michelle, Marianne, Sherry, Heather, and all my other wonderful friends who don't fall into exact text thread categories—You are my people. You're also excellent content, and that alone keeps me coming back for more. But more than that, you're crazy fun, unpredictable, sometimes even outrageous—and I wouldn't have it any other way. Thanks for waiting patiently for me every time I chase another one of my wildly ambitious but "totally doable" ideas.

Mom, Dad, Cory, and Curtis—I'm as surprised as you are that I can write complete sentences people want to read. God has shown favor on our family through ministry, memories, and a lifetime of laughter. I'm forever grateful. And yes, as you like to point out, you got thrown under the bus again—because apparently, that's just how I write books. Also, can we please convince Leo's to start throwing sopapillas?

The Esther Press Team—Thank you for believing in me, encouraging me, and publishing my words with only the occasional "Okay, maybe tone *that* part down." Susan, Stephanie, and Annette, you champion authors in a way that makes us feel seen and valued. And to Andrea, my editor—thank you for hating the word *things* and your firm ban on me talking about writing the book *in* the book. You made me better in every chapter.

Erik Wolgemuth (I nailed the spelling this time)—I had no idea what a gem I was getting when you agreed to be my agent. Thank you for your wisdom, calm confidence, and for being the kindest, most reassuring presence in every Zoom room you enter. It's a gift.

Notes

Chapter 1

1. NLI Staff, "The Neuroscience of Storytelling," NeuroLeadership Institute, September 30, 2021, https://neuroleadership.com/your-brain-at-work/the-neuroscience-of-storytelling.

2. "Studies Confirm the Power of Visuals to Engage Your Audience in eLearning," SH!FT, accessed July 16, 2025, www.shiftelearning.com/blog/bid/350326/studies-confirm-the-power-of-visuals-in-elearning.

3. Riley Seymour, "How Bamboo Grows," Cozy Earth, August 29, 2022, https://cozyearth.com/blogs/news/how-bamboo-grows.

4. Mark Batterson, "Jesus: The Power of a Seed–Dr. Mark Batterson," June 25, 2023, by National Community Church, YouTube, 38:38, www.youtube.com/watch?v=kI0hXUo5Tw0

5. Attributed to Warren Buffett, 2006 Berkshire Hathaway Shareholder Meeting, www.youtube.com/shorts/LgfLiTj89uw.

Chapter 2

1. Mendy Hecht, "The 613 Commandments (Mitzvot)," Chabad.org, accessed July 15, 2025, www.chabad.org/library/article_cdo/aid/756399/jewish/The-613-Commandments-Mitzvot.htm.

2. Amy Eley, "Craig Melvin to Join Savannah Guthrie as TODAY Co-anchor in January 2025," Today, updated November 14, 2024, www.today.com/news/craig-melvin-co-anchor-today-show-january-2025-rcna180107.

Chapter 3

1. Madeleine L'Engle, *A Wind in the Door* (Square Fish, 2007), 88.

Chapter 5

1. Phie Jacobs, "Tickled Rats Reveal Brain Structure That Controls Laughter," Science, July 28, 2023, www.science.org/content/article/tickled-rats-reveal-brain-structure-controls-laughter.

2. "Colonoscopy Overview," Guy's and St Thomas' NHS, last reviewed April 2025, www.guysandstthomas.nhs.uk/health-information/colonoscopy.

3. Darren Orf, "Without Landmarks, Humans Can't Walk in a Straight Line," Interesting Facts, accessed July 15, 2025, https://interestingfacts.com/fact/without-landmarks-humans-cant-walk-in-a-straight-line.

Chapter 6

1. Bryan Parys, "Why Taylor Swift Is So Popular (Berklee's Version)," Berklee, accessed September 8, 2025, www.berklee.edu/berklee-now/news/taylor-swifts-global-popularity-explained-berklees-version.

2. Steven Furtick, "The Prison of Offense," posted August 15, 2016, by Elevation Church, YouTube, 6:09, www.youtube.com/watch?v=RwXqcOMw0ng.

3 . Lewis B. Smedes, *Forgive and Forget: Healing the Hurts We Don't Deserve* (New York: Harper & Row, 1984).

4. Warren Wiersbe, *The Wiersbe Bible Commentary: New Testament* (Colorado Springs, CO: David C Cook, 2007), 20.

Chapter 8

1. Khaleda Rahman, "Tribute in the Sky [...]" Daily Mail UK, March 30, 2016, www.dailymail.co.uk/news/article-3515781/Tribute-sky-Loving-brother-turns-journey-Southwest-Airlines-visit-terminally-ill-sister-party-celebrating-life-flight-attendant.html.

2. "21 Extraordinary Stories of Generosity That Will Stay with You," *Reader's Digest*, November 4, 2022, www.rd.com/article/extraordinary-generosity.

3. Yasaman Nourkhalaj, "Why Giving Is Good for Your Health (and Not Just for the Holidays)," Stanford, January 24, 2025, https://longevity.stanford.edu/lifestyle/2025/01/24/why-giving-is-good-for-your-health.

Chapter 9

1. Craig Groeschel, "A Matter of Integrity," posted by Life Church, May 16, 2021, YouTube, 10:40, www.youtube.com/watch?v=bc7NNocPNHc.

Chapter 10

1. "FULL SHOW: Tom Brady's Patriots Hall of Fame Induction Ceremony," posted by New England Patriots, June 14, 2024, YouTube, 2:52:20, www.youtube.com/watch?v=5XpFfyG_hx4&t=3570s.

Chapter 11

1. Brigham Young University, "Flourishing Romances Are More the Result of Proactive Behaviors Than Soulmate Spark, Study Finds," Phys.org, April 5, 2024, https://phys.org/news/2024-04-flourishing-romances-result-proactive-behaviors.html?utm_source=chatgpt.com.

Chapter 12

1. "Goodness of God," featuring Jenn Johnson, on *Victory*, Bethel Music, 2019.

Chapter 14

1. "Via Dolorosa," featuring Sandi Patty, on *Songs from the Heart*, Capitol CMG, 1983.

2. Arthur C. Brooks, "This Holiday Season, We Can All Learn a Lesson from Beethoven," *Washington Post*, December 13, 2019, www.washingtonpost.com/opinions/this-holiday-season-we-can-all-learn-a-lesson-from-beethoven/2019/12/13/71f21aba-1d0e-11ea-b4c1-fd0d91b60d9e_story.html.

Chapter 15

1. "Carbonated Soft Drinks Global Report," Business Research Co., January 2025, www.thebusinessresearchcompany.com/report/carbonated-soft-drinks-global-market-report.

2. Jack Caporal, "Average American Household Debt in 2025: Facts and Figures," Motley Fool Money, updated August 6, 2025, www.fool.com/money/research/average-household-debt.

3. Jacqueline Zote, "26 Instagram Stats You Need to Know for 2025," Sprout Social, February 21, 2025, https://sproutsocial.com/insights/instagram-stats.

4. Matthew A. McIntosh, "Christianity's Decline in the Western World Continues at More Rapid Pace," Brewminate, July 28, 2023, https://brewminate.com/christianitys-decline-in-the-western-world-continues-at-more-rapid-pace.

5. Michelle Zhang, "Not Enough Time in the Day: Exploring How Busy Schedules Affect Americans' Sleep," Zoma Sleep, October 25, 2023, https://zomasleep.com/blog/not-enough-time-in-the-day-exploring-how-busy-schedules-affect-americans-sleep.

6. Cynthia Yanof, host, *MESSmerized*, podcast, season 1, episode 33, "What's Your Next 'Yes' for 2024? with Pastor Libin Abraham," January 3, 2024, 41:12, https://cynthiayanof.com/whats-your-next-yes-for-2024-with-pastor-libin-abraham.

7. Simon Sinek, "How Great Leaders Inspire Action," TED Talk, Puget Sound, September 2009, www.ted.com/talks/simon_sinek_how_great_leaders_inspire_action.

8. Sinek, "Great Leaders," 12:57.

Chapter 16

1. "'This Is the Worst Pain Any Human Has Ever Felt,' Man with Flu Tells Wife Who Pushed 3 Children Out of Body," *Babylon Bee*, January 19, 2023, https://babylonbee.com/news/this-is-the-worst-pain-any-human-has-ever-felt-man-with-flu-tells-wife-who-pushed-3-children-out-of-body.

2. Louie Giglio, "The Miracle and the Message pt. 2," posted by Passion Equip, April 17, 2024, YouTube, www.youtube.com/watch?v=RWn1OjExAkw.

3. Giglio, "The Miracle," 40:32.

Chapter 17

1. *Merriam-Webster*, s.v. "arise," accessed July 16, 2025, www.merriam-webster.com/dictionary/arise.

Chapter 18: Your Own Personal Mount Rushmore

1. "Mount Rushmore: Student Guide," National Park Service, updated January 30, 2023, www.nps.gov/moru/learn/kidsyouth/student-guide.htm.

2. "Mount Rushmore: Student Guide."

3. Dallas Willard, *The Spirit of the Disciplines: Understanding How God Changes Lives* (San Francisco: HarperCollins, 2009), 6.